THE
DELL BOOK
OF
LOGIC
PROBLEMS #5

THE
DELL BOOK
OF
LOGIC
PROBLEMS #5

Editor-in-Chief • Erica L. Rothstein
Special Editor • Kathleen Reineke
Senior Editor • Theresa Turner

A DELL TRADE PAPERBACK

A DELL TRADE PAPERBACK

Published by
Dell Publishing
a division of
Bantam Doubleday Dell Publishing Group, Inc.
1540 Broadway
New York, New York 10036

ISBN: 0-440-50298-5

Printed in the United States of America
Published simultaneously in Canada

November 1992

10   9   8   7

KPP

A WORD ABOUT THIS BOOK

Caed Mille Failte! is an old Irish greeting which means "a hundred thousand welcomes." That is what we want to wish you—*Caed Mille Failte* to this, the fifth in the paperback book series of Dell Logic Problems. Awaiting you within the pages of this book are 75 brand-new Logic Problems, created by the world's best constructors for your solving pleasure.

For those of you who are new to Logic Problems, a special welcome to this unique kind of puzzle solving, where all the information needed to solve is included in the problem itself—no bulky reference works to carry around, no trips to the library to research some esoteric piece of information. As it says in the How-to-Solve section that begins on page 13, "The Logic Problems in this book are just that— problems based on logic, to which you need bring no specialized knowledge or extensive vocabulary. All you need is your common sense [and] some reasoning power. . . ." Information about how to use the various charts that are provided with most puzzles is given in clear, step-by-step instructions, so you can begin to solve almost immediately, even if you have never solved a Logic Problem before opening this book.

For those of you who are old hands at solving Logic Problems, we don't have to remind you of the stimulating fun that awaits you on the pages that follow. It's been quite a while since you've faced the prospect of tackling 75 never-before-published Logic Problems. They're here, just waiting to give you hours and hours and hours of puzzle-solving fun; but, then, as we all know, good things come to those who wait. And this, the fifth edition of THE DELL BOOK OF LOGIC PROBLEMS is as good as it gets. Only the finest puzzles, by the world's greatest constructors, brought together by the best editors in puzzledom are good enough for the greatest solvers in the world—you. If that sounds like a lot of superlatives, it is, but this book, and you, deserve every one of them!

Once you've taken this book home with you and gotten involved with it (and we have no doubt that you will get *seriously* involved!), take a few minutes to let us know how you liked it. We're all solvers here, too, and the opinions of fellow solvers are highly thought of in these editorial offices.

The only thing left to say to all solvers is, "Grab your pencil and start solving."

THE EDITORS
Dell Book of Logic Problems #5
Dell Puzzle Magazines
1540 Broadway
New York, New York 10036

A LETTER FROM THE EDITOR

No one who works in the puzzle field toils in complete isolation. That's especially true when it comes to Logic Problems. The 20 craftsmen who constructed the puzzles in this book (we call them "constructors" because a puzzle is just that— a thing whose elements are put together systematically) certainly do so in the privacy of their own homes, but then remand their handiwork into the custody of editors. These editors solve the puzzles, determining each puzzle's level of difficulty, checking to make sure that the logic is sound and that the deductive reasoning used to arrive at the solution is explained in such a way that the solver who is stuck can understand each and every step involved in the process. No easy task, I assure you. Writing, rewriting, and re-solving takes place over and over again, until each puzzle is as perfect as skilled professionals can make it. After typesetting, a proofreader (or two or three) check to make sure that there were no errors made by the typesetter and again that each problem's logic does evolve properly.

These skilled professionals rarely get the credit they deserve. It should be noted, of course, that solvers could not possibly be expected to know or understand the degree to which their solving enjoyment is dependent on the devotion puzzle folk give to their work. Devotion is the right word, too, because this is as much a labor of love as it is a job. Stacey E. Feinman and Gail Accardi have for over seven years given themselves to producing the very best puzzles money can buy. That the puzzles in this book are as good as they are owes much to both of them. Peter Levine, a newcomer to the puzzle field, has shown a knack for solving Logic Problems and that, too, is reflected herein. Fran Hendon, one-time editor here at the Dell Puzzle Magazines, has spent much of the last 40 years proofreading. We depend upon her awesome ability to root out the minute inconsistencies that could leave solvers pulling out their hair in frustration; we really would not know what to do without her.

All that notwithstanding, solvers ultimately get the most credit—because it is up to you to recognize quality. Clearly, you do recognize it, for the name Dell has been synonymous with quality puzzles for over 60 years. The only way to recognize that quality, though, is to solve . . . and that is just what, without further ado, you should get busy doing!

ERICA L. ROTHSTEIN
Editor-in-Chief
Dell Puzzle Magazines

CONTENTS

EASY LOGIC PROBLEMS

MEDIUM LOGIC PROBLEMS

HARD LOGIC PROBLEMS

CHALLENGER LOGIC PROBLEMS

Solutions begin on page 133.

HOW TO SOLVE LOGIC PROBLEMS

For those of you who are new to Logic Problems: On the following pages you will find some insights into the thought processes that go into solving these puzzles, as well as detailed instructions on the use of charts as solving aids. We suggest you scan these instructions to familiarize yourself with the techniques presented here. Whenever you feel that you're ready to try your hand at solving, turn to the first puzzle (which you will find on page 25) and dig right in. If, even after you have studied these instructions, you should find yourself stuck while solving, turn to the solution for that puzzle and try to follow the reasoning given there. The solutions are not just a listing of "who did what," but rather a step-by-step elimination of possibilities, which you should find invaluable on your journey along the road to mastery of Logic Problems.

The 75 Logic Problems in this book are just that—problems based on logic, to which you need bring no specialized knowledge or extensive vocabulary. Instead, all you will need is your common sense, some reasoning power, and a basic grasp of how to use the charts or other solving aids provided. The problems themselves are all classic deduction problems, in which you are usually asked to figure out how two or more sets of facts relate to each other—what first name belongs with which last name, for example. All of the facts you will need to solve each puzzle are always given.

The puzzles are mostly arranged in increasing order of difficulty—the first few are rather easy to solve, then the puzzles get more difficult as you continue through the book. The final puzzles are especially challenging. If you are new to Logic Problems, we suggest that you start with the first puzzles, progressing through the book as you get more expert at solving.

Of the three examples which follow, the first is, of course, the most basic, but the skills utilized there will help you tackle even the most challenging challenger. Example #2 will help you hone those skills and gives valuable hints about the use of a more complicated chart as a solving aid. The third member of the group will introduce those puzzles for which the normal solving chart is not applicable. You will notice that in each of these examples, as in all the Logic Problems in this book, the last part of the introduction will tell you what facts you are to establish in solving that puzzle. Now, if you are ready to begin, read through the introduction and the clues given with Example #1.

EXAMPLE #1

A young woman attending a party was introduced to four men in rather rapid succession and, as usual at such gatherings, their respective types of work were mentioned rather early in the conversation. Unfortunately, she was afflicted with a somewhat faulty memory. Half an hour later, she could remember only that she had met a Mr. Brown, a Mr. White, a Mr. Black, and a Mr. Green. She recalled that among them were a photographer, a grocer, a banker, and a singer, but she could not recall which was which. Her hostess, a fun-loving friend, refused to refresh her memory, but offered four clues. Happily, the young woman's logic was better than her memory, and she quickly paired each man with his profession. Can you? Here are the clues:

1. Mr. White approached the banker for a loan.

2. Mr. Brown had met the photographer when he hired him to take pictures of his wedding.

3. The singer and Mr. White are friends, but have never had business dealings.

4. Neither Mr. Black nor the singer had ever met Mr. Green before that evening.

	Black	Brown	Green	White
banker				
grocer				
photo.			.	
singer				

You know from the last part of the introduction what it is you are to determine— you are to match each man's last name with his profession. The chart has been set up to help you keep track of the information as you discover it. We suggest that you use an X in a box to indicate a definite impossibility and a • (dot) in a box to show an established fact.

Your first step is to enter X's into the chart for all of the obvious possibilities that you can see from information given in the clues. It is apparent from clue 1 that Mr. White is not the banker, so an X would be entered into the White/banker box. Clue 2 makes it clear that Mr. Brown is not the photographer, so another X in the Brown/ photographer box can be entered. Clue 3 tells you that Mr. White is not the singer. And from clue 4 you can see that neither Mr. Black nor Mr. Green is the singer. Each of these impossibilities should also be indicated by X's in the chart. Once you have done so, your chart will look like this:

	Black	Brown	Green	White
banker				X
grocer				
photo.		X		
singer	X		X	X

Remembering that each X indicates that something is *not* a fact, note the row of boxes at the bottom—corresponding to which of the men is the singer. There are four possibilities, and you have X's for three of them. Therefore, Mr. Brown, the only one left, has to be the singer. Put a dot (•) in the singer/Brown box. Also, remember that if Mr. Brown is the singer, he is not the photographer (which we knew, we have an X); and he cannot be the grocer or the banker either. Thus, you would put X's in those boxes too. Your chart would now look like this:

	Black	Brown	Green	White
banker		X		X
grocer		X		
photo.		X		
singer	X	•	X	X

Now you seem to have a "hopeless" situation! You have used all the clues, and you have matched one man with his profession—but the additional X's entered in the chart do not enable you to make another match, since the possibilities have not been narrowed down sufficiently. What to do next?

Your next step is to reread the clues, at the same time considering the new information you have acquired: You know that Mr. Brown is the singer and that he has done business with the photographer (clue 2). But the singer has never done business with Mr. White (clue 3) or with Mr. Green (clue 4). And that means that neither Mr. White nor Mr. Green can possibly be the photographer. You can now place X's in those boxes in the chart. After you have done so, here is what you will have:

	Black	Brown	Green	White
banker		X		X
grocer		X		•
photo.	•	X	X	X
singer	X	•	X	X

And you see that you do have more answers! The photographer must be Mr. Black, since there are X's in the boxes for the other names. Mr. White, also, must be the grocer, since there is an X in the other three boxes under his name. Once you have placed a dot to indicate that Mr. Black is the photographer and a dot to show that Mr. White is the grocer (always remembering to place X's in the other boxes in the row and column that contain the dot) your chart will look like this:

	Black	Brown	Green	White
banker	X	X		X
grocer	X	X	X	•
photo.	•	X	X	X
singer	X	•	X	X

You can see that you are left with one empty box, and this box corresponds to the remaining piece of information you have not yet determined—what Mr. Green's profession is and who the banker is. Obviously, the only possibility is that Mr. Green is the banker. And the Logic Problem is solved!

Most of the Logic Problems in this book will ask you to determine how more than two sets of facts are related to each other. You'll see, however, that the way of solving a more involved Logic Problem is just the same as Example #1—*if* you have a grasp of how to make the best use of the solving chart. The next example of a Logic Problem is presented in order to explain how to use a bigger chart. As before, read through the problem quickly, noting that the introduction tells you what facts you are to determine.

EXAMPLE #2

Andy, Chris, Noel, Randy, and Steve—one of whose last name is Morse—were recently hired as refreshment vendors at Memorial Stadium; each boy sells only one kind of fare. From the clues below, try to determine each boy's full name and the type of refreshment he sells.

1. Randy, whose last name is not Wiley, does not sell popcorn.

2. The Davis boy does not sell soda or candy.

3. The five boys are Noel, Randy, the Smith boy, the Coble boy, and the boy who sells ice cream.

4. Andy's last name is not Wiley or Coble. Neither Andy nor Coble is the boy who sells candy.

5. Neither the peanut vendor nor the ice cream vendor is named Steve or Davis.

	Coble	Davis	Morse	Smith	Wiley	candy	ice.	pean.	pop.	soda
Andy										
Chris										
Noel										
Randy										
Steve										
candy										
ice.										
pean.										
pop.										
soda										

Note that the chart given is composed of three sets of boxes—one set corresponding to the first and last names; a second set (to the right) corresponding to first names and refreshment; and a third set, below the first set, corresponding to the refreshment and last names. Notice, too, that these sets are separated from each other by heavier lines so that it is easier to find the particular box you are looking for.

As in Example #1, your first step is to enter into the boxes of the chart the impossibilities. Keep in mind that you have many more boxes to be concerned with here. Remember, ROW indicates the boxes that go horizontally (the Andy row, for example) and the word COLUMN indicates the boxes that go vertically (the Coble column, for instance).

Clue 1 tells you that Randy's last name is not Wiley, and Randy does not sell popcorn. Thus, enter an X into the Randy/Wiley box and another X in the Randy/popcorn box in the Randy row. Clue 2 says that the Davis boy sells neither soda nor candy. Find Davis and go down that column to the Davis/soda box and put an X in it; then find the Davis/candy box in that same column and place an X in that box.

Clue 3 tells you a few things: It gives you all five of the boys, either by his first name (two of them), his last name (another two of them), or by what refreshment he sells (the remaining boy). You then know something about all five—one boy's first name is Noel, another's is Randy; a third boy has the last name Smith, a fourth has the last name Coble; and the fifth sells ice cream. All of these are different people. So, in the chart you have a lot of X's that can be entered. Noel's last name is neither Smith nor Coble, so enter X's in the Noel/Smith, Noel/Coble boxes; nor can Noel be the ice cream seller, so put an X in the Noel/ice cream box. Randy is neither Smith nor Coble, and Randy does not sell ice cream, so put the X's in the Randy/Smith, Randy/Coble, and Randy/ice cream boxes. And neither Smith nor Coble sells ice cream, so enter an X in those two boxes.

Clue 4 tells you that Andy's last name is neither Wiley nor Coble. It also says that Andy does not sell candy and neither does the Coble boy. By now you probably know where to put the X's—in the Andy/Wiley box, the Andy/Coble box, the Andy/candy box, and in the box in the Coble column corresponding to candy. From clue 5 you learn that neither Steve nor Davis is the boy who sells either peanuts or ice cream. (One important point here—read clue 5 again, and note that this clue does *not* tell you whether or not Steve's last name is Davis; it tells you only that neither the peanut seller nor the ice cream vendor has the first name Steve or the last name Davis.) Your chart should now look like this:

	Coble	Davis	Morse	Smith	Wiley	candy	ice.	pean.	pop.	soda
Andy	X				X	X				
Chris										
Noel	X			X			X			
Randy	X			X	X		X		X	
Steve							X	X		
candy	X	X			
ice.	X	X		X	
pean.		X			
pop.					
soda		X			

From this point on, we suggest that you fill in the above chart yourself as you read how the facts are established. If you look at the Davis column, you will see that you have X's in four of the refreshment boxes; the Davis boy is the one who sells popcorn. Put a dot in the Davis/popcorn box. Now, since it is Davis who sells popcorn, none of the other boys does, so you will put X's in all of the other boxes in that popcorn row.

Your next step will be to look up at the other set of refreshment boxes and see what first names already have an X in the popcorn column. Note that Randy has an X in the popcorn column (from clue 1). Thus, if you know that Randy does not sell popcorn, you now know that his last name is not Davis, since Davis is the popcorn seller. You can then put an X in the Randy/Davis box. After you've done this, you'll see that you now have four X's for Randy's last name. Randy has to be Morse, the only name left, so enter a dot in the Randy/Morse box. Don't forget, too, to enter X's in the boxes of the Morse column that correspond to the first names of the other boys.

Now that you know Randy is Morse, you are ready to look at what you've already discovered about Randy and transfer that information to the Morse column—remember that since Randy is Morse, anything that you know about Randy is also true of Morse, as they're the same person. You'll see that an X for Randy was entered from clue 3: Randy does not sell ice cream. Then Morse cannot be the ice cream seller either, so put an X in the Morse column to show that Morse doesn't sell ice cream.

Once the Morse/ice cream X is in place, note what you have established about the Wiley boy: His is the only last name left who can sell ice cream. Put the dot in the Wiley/ice cream box and enter X's in the Wiley column for all the other refreshments. Your next step? As before, you are ready to determine what this new dot will tell you, so you will go up to the other set of refreshment boxes and see what you have established about the ice cream vendor. He's not Noel or Steve—they have two X's already entered in the chart. Now that you have established the Wiley boy as the ice cream seller, you know that his first name can't be either Noel or Steve because neither of those boys sells ice cream. Once you've put X's in the Noel/Wiley box and the Steve/Wiley box, you'll see that you know who Wiley is. Remember that clue 4 had already told you that Andy's last name is not Wiley, so you have an X in the Andy/Wiley box. With the new X's, do you see that Wiley's first name has to be Chris? And since Chris is Wiley, and Wiley sells ice cream, so, of course, does Chris. Thus, you can put a dot in the Chris/ice cream box. And don't forget to put X's in the Chris row for the other refreshments and also in the ice cream column for the other first names.

Notice that once Chris Wiley is entered in the chart, there are now four X's in the Coble column, and Steve is the one who has to be the Coble boy. Put in the dot and then X's in the Steve row, and your chart looks like this:

	Coble	Davis	Morse	Smith	Wiley	candy	ice.	pean.	pop.	soda
Andy	X		X		X	X	X			
Chris	X	X	X	X	•	X	•	X	X	X
Noel	X		X	X	X		X			
Randy	X	X	•	X	X		X		X	
Steve	•	X	X	X	X		X	X		
candy	X	X			X					
ice.	X	X	X	X	•					
pean.		X			X					
pop.	X	•	X	X	X					
soda		X			X					

See that there are four X's in the Smith/first name column, so Smith's first name must be Andy. And Noel's last name is Davis, because he's the only one left. Remember—look down the Davis row and see that we already know Davis sells popcorn. So, Noel, whose last name is Davis, sells popcorn. And, of course, there should be X's in all the other boxes of the Noel row and the popcorn column.

Now that you have completely established two sets of facts—which first name goes with which last name—you can use the two sets of refreshment boxes almost as one. That is, since you know each boy's first name and last name, anything you have determined about a first name will hold true for that boy's last name; and, naturally, the reverse is true: whatever you know about a boy's last name must also be true of that boy's first name.

For example, you know that Coble is Steve, so look down the Coble column and note that you have already put X's in the candy, ice cream, and popcorn boxes. Go up to the Steve row and enter any X's that you know about Coble. After putting an X in the Steve/candy box, you'll see that you've determined that Steve sells soda. As always, don't forget to enter X's where appropriate once you've entered a dot to indicate a determined fact. These X's are what will narrow down the remaining possibilities.

Things are really moving fast now! Once you've entered the appropriate X's in the Steve row and the soda column, you will quickly see that there are four X's in the candy column—so, Randy (Morse) is the candy vendor. By elimination, Andy (Smith) sells peanuts and this Logic Problem is completely solved.

Many of the Logic Problems in this book will have charts that are set up much like the one in Example #2. They may be bigger, and the puzzle may involve matching more sets of facts, but the method of solving the Logic Problem using the chart will be exactly the same. Just remember:

Always read the whole problem through quickly. What you are to determine is usually stated in the last part of the introduction.

When using solving charts, use an X to indicate a definite impossibility and a • (dot) to indicate an established fact.

Once you have placed a dot to indicate an established fact, remember to put X's in the rest of the boxes in the row and the column that contains the dot.

Every time you establish a fact, it is a good idea to go back and reread the clues, keeping in mind the newly found information. Often, you will find that rereading the clues will help you if you seem to be "stuck." You may discover that you *do* know more facts than you thought you did.

Don't forget, when you establish a fact in one part of a solving chart, check to see if the new information is applicable to any other section of the solving chart—see if some X's or dots can be transferred from one section to another.

Just one other note before we get to Example #3, and this note applies to both the most inexperienced novice and the most experienced expert. If ever you find yourself stymied while solving a problem, don't get discouraged and give up—turn to the solution. Read the step-by-step elimination until you get to a fact that you have not established and see if you can follow the reasoning given. By going back and forth between the clue numbers cited in the solution and the clues themselves, you should be able to "get over the hump" and still have the satisfaction of completing the rest of the puzzle by yourself. Sometimes reading the solution of one puzzle will give you important clues (if you'll pardon the pun) to the thought processes involved with many other puzzles. And now to the last of our trio of examples.

Sometimes a Logic Problem has been created in such a way that the type of chart you learned about in Example #2 is not helpful in solving the problem. The puzzle itself is fine, but another kind of chart—a fill-in type—will better help you match up the facts and arrive at the correct solution. Example #3 is a puzzle using this type of solving chart.

EXAMPLE #3

It was her first visit home in ten years, and Louise wondered how she would manage to see her old friends and still take in the things she wanted to in the seven days she had to spend there. Her worry was needless, however, for when she got off the plane Sunday morning, there were her friends—Anna, Cora, Gert, Jane, Liz, and Mary—waiting to greet her with her seven-day visit all planned. The women knew that Louise wanted to revisit the restaurant where they always used to have lunch together, so Louise's vacation began that Sunday afternoon with a party. After that, each of the women had an entire day to spend with Louise, accompanying her to one of the following things: a ball game, concert, the theater, museum, zoo, and one day reserved for just shopping. From the clues below, find out who took Louise where and on what day.

1. Anna and the museum visitor and the woman whose day followed the zoo visitor were blondes; Gert and the concertgoer and the woman who spent Monday with Louise were brunettes. *(Note: All six women are mentioned in this clue.)*

2. Cora's day with Louise was not the visit that occurred the day immediately following Mary's day.

3. The six women visited with Louise in the following order: Jane was with Louise the day after the zoo visitor and four days before the museumgoer; Gert was with Louise the day after the theatergoer and the day before Mary.

4. Anna and the woman who took Louise shopping have the same color hair.

	Monday	Tuesday	Wednesday	Thursday	Friday	Saturday
friend						
activity						

As before (and always) read the entire puzzle through quickly. Note that here you are to determine which day, from Monday to Saturday, each woman spent with Louise and also what they did that day. The solving chart, often called a fill-in chart, is the best kind to use for this puzzle. You won't be entering X's and dots here; instead, you will be writing the facts into the chart as you determine them and also find out where they belong.

From clue 1 you can eliminate both Anna and Gert as the woman who took Louise to the museum and the concert. And neither of these activities took place on a Monday, nor did Anna or Gert spend Monday with Louise. You have discovered some things, but none of them can yet be entered into the chart. Most solvers find it useful to note these facts elsewhere, perhaps in the margin or on a piece of scratch paper, in their own particular kind of shorthand. Then when enough facts have been determined to begin writing them into the chart, you will already have them listed.

Do you see that clue 2 tells you Mary did not see Louise on Saturday? It's because the clue states that Cora's day was not the visit that occurred immediately following Mary's day, and thus, there had to be at least one visit after Mary's. You still don't have a definite fact to write into the chart. Don't lose heart, though, because . . .

. . . clue 3 will start to crack the puzzle! Note that this clue gives you the order of the six visits. Since the days were Monday through Saturday, the only possible way for Jane to be with Louise the day after the zoo visitor and four days before the museumgoer is if the zoo visit took place on Monday, Jane was with Louise on Tuesday, and the museumgoer was with Louise on Saturday. These facts can now be written into the chart—Monday zoo, Tuesday Jane, Saturday museum. Three days have been accounted for. The last part of clue 3 gives you the other three days: with Wednesday, Thursday, and Friday still open, the theatergoer must be the Wednesday friend, Gert is the day after, or Thursday, and Mary saw Louise on Friday. These facts, too, should be written in the chart. Once you've done so, your chart will resemble this one:

	Monday	Tuesday	Wednesday	Thursday	Friday	Saturday
friend		Jane		Gert	Mary	
activity	zoo		theater			museum

Now go back to clue 1 and see what other facts you can establish. There are three blondes—Anna, the museum visitor, and the woman whose day followed the zoo visitor's. The chart shows you that this last woman was Jane. From clue 4 you learn that the woman who took Louise shopping and Anna have the same color hair—blond. The woman who took Louise shopping is not Anna (they're two separate people), nor is she the museum visitor, so she must be the woman whose day followed the zoo visitor's, Jane. That fact can be written in the chart.

You can also, at this point, establish what day Anna spent with Louise. Since you know it's not Monday (clue 1) and Anna is not the museumgoer (also clue 1), the only day left for her is Wednesday, so Anna took Louise to the theater. Clue 2 tells you that Cora's day did not immediately follow Mary's, so Cora's day can't be Saturday, and must be Monday. By elimination, Liz (listed in the introduction) spent Saturday with Louise at the museum.

It may be helpful to make a note of the hair colors mentioned in clue 1, perhaps under the relevant columns in the chart. These hair colors can again be used at this point. We've now established the blondes as Anna, Jane, and Liz; the brunettes are Gert, the concertgoer, and Cora. The only possibility is that Mary is the concertgoer. Everything has now been determined except what Gert did, so, by elimination, Gert must have taken Louise to a ball game (from the introduction).

	Monday	Tuesday	Wednesday	Thursday	Friday	Saturday
friend	Cora	Jane	Anna	Gert	Mary	Liz
activity	zoo	shopping	theater	ball game	concert	museum
	bru	blo	blo	bru	bru	blo

Are all Logic Problems easy to solve? No, of course not. Many of the puzzles in this book are much more complicated than the three examples and should take a great deal more time and thought before you arrive at the solution. However, the techniques you use to solve the puzzles are essentially the same. All the information needed to solve will be given in the puzzle itself, either in the introduction or the clues. As you eliminate possibilities, you will narrow down the choices until, finally, you can establish a certainty. That certainty will usually help narrow down the possibilities in another set of facts. Once you have determined something, you will probably need to return to the clues and reread them, keeping in mind what facts you have now established. Suddenly a sentence in the clues may tell you something you could not have determined before, thus narrowing down the choices still further. Eventually you will have determined everything, and the Logic Problem will be solved.

EASY LOGIC PROBLEMS

1 PUMPKIN CARVERS

by Mary Marks Cezus

Sally and three friends each bought a pumpkin at a local produce market. No two people carved their pumpkins to resemble the same object nor did any two buy their pumpkins at the same market. Using the clues below, can you determine each person's name, pumpkin design, and market (one shopped at Autumn Bounty)?

1. Timothy and the person who carved the pumpkin that looked like a moon (which was not purchased at Harvest of Plenty) both shopped on Saturday.

2. The person who carved the pumpkin that looked like a pirate and the person who shopped at Friendly Acres (who was not Roy) both bought very large pumpkins.

3. Neither Timothy nor the person who carved the lion pumpkin shopped at Harvest of Plenty.

4. The person who shopped at The Pie Patch and the person who carved the pumpkin that looked like a pirate both like to roast pumpkin seeds.

5. Patsy (who did not shop at Harvest of Plenty) and the person who carved the pumpkin to resemble a lion both enjoy raking leaves.

6. Neither Timothy nor Roy carved the pumpkin that looked like an owl.

The solution is on page 135.

	lion	moon	owl	pirate	Autumn	Friendly	Harvest	Pie Patch
Patsy	X	O	X	X	X	O	X	X
Roy	O	X	X	X	X	X	X	O
Sally	X	X	O	X	X	X	O	X
Timothy	X	X	X	O	O	X	X	X
Autumn	X	X	X	O				
Friendly	X	O	X	X				
Harvest	X	X	O	X				
Pie Patch	O	X	X	X				

Sally – Owl – Harvest of Plenty

Patsy – Moon

25

2 HALLOWEEN PAGEANT

by Claudia Strong

Four members of the third-grade class of Spooky Hollow Elementary School were featured in a production of that school's annual Halloween pageant. Each of the four classmates was the "star" of one of the four consecutive scenes, and each portrayed a different traditional Halloween character. From the clues below, can you determine which part each child played and the featured player of each scene?

1. The first scene did not star the black cat.

2. Kim (who did not play the part of the pumpkin) was not in Scene 4.

3. Lee came directly after Trent, but earlier in the show than the skeleton.

4. The part of the black cat was not played by Sal.

5. The ghost appeared in the scene immediately after the pumpkin.

The solution is on page 135.

	Sc. I	Sc. II	Sc. III	Sc. IV	cat	ghost	pumpkin	skeleton
Kim	X	X	O	X	O	X	X	X
Lee	X	O	X	X	X	O	X	X
Sal	X	X	X	O	X	X	X	O
Trent	O	X	X	X	X	X	O	X
cat	X	X	O	X				
ghost	X	O	X	X				
pumpkin	O	X	X	X				
skeleton	X	X	X	O				

3 VITAL STATISTICS

by Varda Maslowski

As part of the annual physical given to Ocean Village Industries staffers, the company nurse notes the age, height, and weight of each employee. One morning last week, she examined four male employees, each a different age (one is 20 years old). The four men range in height from 5'8" to 6'2" (one is 6'0"). They vary in weight as well, ranging from 175 to 250 pounds (one weighs 200 pounds). From the following clues, determine the age, height, and weight of the four employees she examined.

1. Alan, who is not 5'10", is younger than Chuck.

2. Bill, who is five years older than Dave, is shorter than the man who weighs 225 pounds.

3. The 35-year-old is four inches taller than the 25-year-old.

4. The shortest man weighs the most; Chuck is not the oldest.

5. The 30-year-old does not weigh the least.

The solution is on page 135.

	20	25	30	35	5'8"	5'10"	6'0"	6'2"	175	200	225	250
Alan												
Bill												
Chuck												
Dave												
175												
200												
225												
250												
5'8"												
5'10"												
6'0"												
6'2"												

4 SNOWY DAY ACTIVITIES

by Diane C. Baldwin

On the first snowy day of winter, Dirk and his brother and sisters (ages 6, 8, 10, and 12) bundle up and rush outside, where each begins a different activity. Their mother, watching out the kitchen window, can easily tell them apart, since each has a different color jacket (one is green). From the clues supplied, can you, too, identify each child by age, activity, and jacket?

1. The oldest child isn't Zoe or the boy who is building the snow fort.

2. The child making the snowman is older than the child in the blue jacket and younger than Rhett.

3. Lana isn't wearing the red jacket; the boy who is shoveling is not the oldest.

4. The child who is sledding is two years older than the one in the yellow jacket, who isn't shoveling snow.

The solution is on page 135.

	shoveling	sledding	snow fort	snowman	blue	green	red	yellow	6	8	10	12
Dirk												
Lana												
Rhett												
Zoe												
6								
8								
10								
12								
blue				
green				
red				
yellow				

28

5 PHONETIC NAMES

by W. H. Organ

The registrar at State College discovered that six of the applicants for admission have unusual names: each whole name sounds like a familiar word or phrase. For example, the applicant from Grass Valley is named John Quill (jonquil). From the following clues, can you determine the full names of the other five, the word or phrase each name forms, the hometown of each (one is Poker Flat) and the language course each plans to take (one is Portuguese)?

1. In addition to Quill, the other surnames are: Hangor, King, Hopper, Dwyer, and Matick. All the first names are: Otto, John, Barb, Claude, Joe, and Cliff. All come from different towns and each plans on taking a different language.

2. Cliff plans to take German. He registered ahead of the student from Templeton, but later in the day than the student from Crestview.

3. Barb is from Tall Palms; Matick from Hilldale. Neither plans to take French.

4. Joe was the last one to register.

5. King plans on taking Russian, Hopper wants to study Spanish.

6. Otto isn't interested in taking Italian.

The solution is on page 136.

Solving hint: Match the names first (don't forget about John Quill from Grass Valley who is mentioned in the introduction). Then use the chart below to fill in the information as you discover it from reading the clues.

first name	last name	hometown	language

6 BALLOON ANIMALS

by Mary A. Powell

Once a week, the students at We Care Nursery School are taken for a special outing. Last Friday, they walked to a nearby park where Violet the Clown gave each child a balloon animal. From the following clues, can you find the full names of the first four children who received balloon animals, and the type of animal and color (one was green) of each child's balloon?

1. Ken's balloon was neither the blue one nor the one shaped like a giraffe.

2. Neither Sara nor the Bradley child received the balloon cat or the red balloon horse.

3. The Johnson child didn't receive the blue balloon.

4. Billy is neither the Bradley child nor the Smith child.

5. The balloon dog was neither the blue nor the yellow animal.

6. Jane is not the King girl.

The solution is on page 136.

	Bradley	Johnson	King	Smith	blue	green	red	yellow	cat	dog	giraffe	horse
Billy												
Jane												
Ken												
Sara												
cat								
dog								
giraffe								
horse								
blue				
green				
red				
yellow				

7 FESTIVAL BOOTHS

by Mary Marks Cezus

The four booths along Festive Lane at the Handiwork Fair each sell a different product. No two booths have the same name, nor do any two have the same color awning. Using the illustration and the clues below, can you determine each booth's position, name (one is "Stardrops"), product, and awning color? ("Left" and "right" in the clues are from the viewpoint of a person facing the booths.)

1. The keychains are to the right of "Just Becuz" and to the left of the yellow awning.

2. The owner of "Brilliance" and the owner of the booth with the blue awning (which is not the second booth) both enjoy crowds.

3. There is exactly one booth between "Magic Door" and the red awning.

4. The silk plants are to the right of the green awning.

5. "Just Becuz" does not sell needlework.

6. The woodcrafts booth is to the right of at least two other booths.

The solution is on page 136.

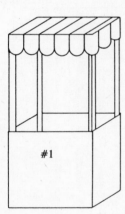

#1

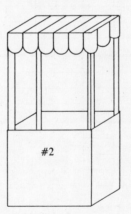

#2

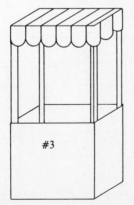

#3

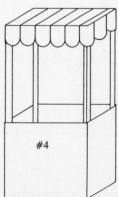

#4

8 EAST-COAST VACATIONS

by Varda Maslowski

The Johnstons and three other couples are planning vacation trips to the East Coast. Each couple is headed for a different destination, including Boston, New York City, Washington, D.C., and Miami Beach. From the following clues, determine the full names of each couple (one wife's name is Carol), along with the city each plans to visit.

1. Anna's destination is north of Ed's, which is north of the Lombard couple's destination.

2. Denise's destination is further north than at least two other couples'; Hank's destination is not the farthest north.

3. Betty's destination is north of Fred's, who is not Mr. Lombard.

4. Anna is not Mrs. Ingersoll; neither Ed nor Gary is Mr. Kline.

The solution is on page 136.

	Ed	Fred	Gary	Hank	Ingersoll	Johnston	Kline	Lombard	Bos.	D.C.	Miami	NYC
Anna												
Betty												
Carol												
Denise												
Boston												
D.C.												
Miami												
NYC												
Ingersoll												
Johnston												
Kline												
Lombard												

This chart might also be of some help.

destination	wife	husband	last name

9 TAKING CARE

by Mary Marks Cezus

Kate and three other mothers were recently discussing their children's day care centers. Each woman has one child and that child's last name is the same as her own. No two women take their children to the same day care centers. Using the clues below, can you determine each woman's first name, her child's first name, their last name (one is Upshaw), and the name of the child's day care center?

1. Neither Margaret's son (whose last name is not Simpson) nor Crystal attends the Small Wonder center.

2. Mrs. Rich (who does not take her child to Lovin' Care) and Norma (whose child is not Anthony) both are very pleased with the care their children are receiving.

3. Brett, the child whose last name is Talman, and Lois's child do not attend Tots Haven.

4. Denise (who is not Simpson) and the child who attends Small Wonder (who is not Lois's child) have fun when they play together.

5. Margaret (who is not Anthony's mother) and the woman who takes her child to Kinder Kindness (who is not Mrs. Talman) both think the fees are reasonable.

The solution is on page 137.

		CHILDREN											
		Anthony	Brett	Crystal	Denise	Rich	Simpson	Talman	Upshaw	KK	LC	SW	TH
MOTHERS	Kate												
	Lois												
	Margaret												
	Norma												
	KK												
	LC												
	SW												
	TH												
	Rich												
	Simpson												
	Talman												
	Upshaw												

33

10   SWEETS TO THE SWEET

by Susan Zivich

*Willkommen** to the annual Swiss candy festival that features the nation's top confections. From the following clues, can you determine each candy maker's full name (one first name is Bert, and one last name is Luzi), the town where each lives, and the chocolate and marzipan creations each displayed?

1. Kurt Scherer is not from Andeer.

2. Rolfe made the marzipan toys.

3. Herr Hassler lives in Donath.

4. Otto made the chocolate swans, and the man from Splugen made the chocolate bunnies.

5. Urs lives in Scharans.

6. The chocolatier who made the roses also made the marzipan animals.

7. Herr Tobler, who is not Rolfe, made the chocolate chalet.

8. Herr Iselin made the marzipan clowns and the man from Zillis made the marzipan elves.

9. Kurt and Urs worked together the day before the festival. One made chocolate butterflies and the other made marzipan fruit.

*Welcome

The solution is on page 137.

Because of the size of this chart, it had to be divided in two, but it is used in the normal way for solving.

	Bert	Kurt	Otto	Rolfe	Urs	And.	Don.	Sch.	Spl.	Zil.	chocolate				
											bunny	butter.	chal.	rose	swan
Hassler															
Iselin															
Luzi															
Scherer															
Tobler															
marzipan animal															
marzipan clown															
marzipan elf															
marzipan fruit															
marzipan toys															
chocolate bunny															
chocolate butter.															
chocolate chalet															
chocolate rose															
chocolate swan															
Andeer															
Donath															
Scharans															
Splugen															
Zillis															

	marzipan				
	animal	clown	elf	fruit	toys
Hassler					
Iselin					
Luzi					
Scherer					
Tobler					

11   FORTUNE SEEKERS

by W. H. Organ

The discovery of gold in California attracted fortune seekers from all over the world. In the fall of 1849, six arrived in the bustling town of Goldville. They had little luck in their mining efforts but, being enterprising young men, each one established his own business which soon prospered in the growing community. From the following clues, can you determine their full names (one first name was Hal and one surname was Maloney), their nationalities (one was Italian), and the businesses they established (one was a restaurant)?

1. Bob, the one who established the livery stable, and the Irishman all arrived in California by ship from South America. Peron, the Dutchman, and the one who started a barber shop all arrived overland by the same wagon train.

2. Meer, who established the grocery store, took a ship only as far as New York. He and Joe Ricardo traveled the rest of the way together.

3. Paul started a laundry service.

4. The Scotsman started a foundry.

5. Cal Wilson is a Welshman.

6. Tim and Burns arrived by ship.

7. The Frenchman's business was next to Joe's.

The solution is on page 137.

The fill-in chart below was found to be most useful in keeping track of the information given in the clues.

first name	last name	nationality	business

12   FINE ARTISTS

by Jean M. Hannagan

The five people who reached the finals in this year's State Arts Festival contest happen to specialize in five different areas—charcoal drawings, portraits, sculpture, seascapes, and still lifes. Each is from a different town in the state, one of which is Midland. One last name is Gold and one first name is Andy. From the following clues, can you discover the full names, specialties, and home towns of the first-, second-, and third-prize winners, and the two artists who received honorable mentions?

1. Adele and the artist from Southlawn both placed ahead of the sculptor, but not as high as the person who does charcoal drawings.

2. Although artists Black and Brown have been contestants for several years, this is the first time either has reached the finals.

3. The artist from Weston, who did not receive the second honorable mention, does not work in charcoal.

4. Arty won a prize higher than that received by the still-life artist; the artist from Northville placed ahead of both, but did not win first prize.

5. The first honorable mention went to the artist from Eastburg, whose name is not Black.

6. Ann and the portrait painter met when they were contestants in last year's finals; this year, they were delighted to meet the artist from Weston, a newcomer to the contest.

7. The charcoal artist placed ahead of the contestant named White.

8. Alice, who is not from Northville, was not the first prize winner (whose last name is not Gray).

The solution is on page 138.

	first name	last name	artwork	town
1st Place				
2nd Place				
3rd Place				
1st Hon. Men.				
2nd Hon. Men.				

MEDIUM LOGIC PROBLEMS

13 NEW PERFUME

by W. H. Organ

The laboratory at the Darling Cosmetic Company has just come up with a terrific new scent. Management, hoping to capitalize as soon as possible on this exciting new product, is busy seeking a name for it. In a company-wide competition, six ideas submitted by employees have been chosen as potential names (one was *Amber*) for the new perfume. From the following clues, can you determine the full names of the employees (one surname is Gamble and one first name is Tom), the department in which each works (all are different—one is Supply), and the name each submitted for the perfume?

1. Sally and the employee who suggested the name *Evening Star* are in the same carpool as Downs.

2. Juan and the employee from the Research Department take a bus to work. The employee who works in Administration is happy that he is able to walk to work.

3. Harry works in Marketing; he suggested the name *Mystique*.

4. Carl Hart suggested the name *Pixie*.

5. Booth does not ride a bus to work; she is in Personnel.

6. Nell, whose last name is not Carroll, does not ride in the car pool. She suggested the name *Foofu*.

7. Evans rides a bus; he works in Finance.

8. *Moon Mist* was not the name suggested by Juan.

The solution is on page 138.

Employee	Perfume	Department

14 HOUSE OF GARDENS

by David Champlin

Each of the five Garden children has his or her own room, which is painted a different color than the rooms of his or her siblings. Each child has a different poster hanging in his or her room (one features Cricketman), and each also has a different collection on display (one girl collects picture postcards). From the information given below, determine the color of each child's room, and the poster and collection each child keeps.

1. Flora does not collect butterflies or teddy bears.

2. The child who lives in the blue room (who is not the oldest) is older than both the child who has the poster of Scarfield the Cat and the one who collects comic books.

3. Herb has two older sisters—one lives in the lavender room and the other has the poster of singer Whitney Dallas.

4. The youngest (who does not collect stamps or teddy bears) has the poster of rock star Alton Jon in her room, which is not painted yellow.

5. Basil does not collect teddy bears or butterflies, and does not live in the green room.

6. Daisy is older than both the comic book collector and Violet, but younger than one of her brothers (who does not have the He-Boy poster in his room).

7. Neither of the boys lives in the pink or yellow room.

The solution is on page 138.

The solution is on page 138.

	blue	green	lavender	pink	yellow	Cricket	Cat	Dallas	He-Boy	Jon	butter.	comics	postc.	stamps	teddys
Basil															
Daisy															
Flora															
Herb															
Violet															
butter.															
comics															
postcards															
stamps															
teddys															
Cricket															
Cat															
Dallas															
He-Boy															
Jon															

15 MAY BASKETS

by Julie Spence

As children, Judy Wilks and five of her friends, including Barb, always exchanged May Day baskets filled with wildflowers and sweets. Now all six are grown women living in different states (one of Judy's friends lives in Alaska). Remembering how much fun it was to receive these baskets, on May 1st last year Judy wired Barb and her other childhood friends surprise May Day baskets, each filled with a different kind of flower (one was a basket of roses). From the information below, can you determine each friend's full name (one is Kohn), the state where each lives, and the kind of flowers each received on May 1st?

1. Four of the five are Susan, Ms. Little, the one who received carnations, and the one who lives in Montana (who is not Jane).

2. Jane, who is not Ms. Little, received tulips.

3. Ms. Thompson, who lives in California, received violets.

4. The one who lives in Ohio did not receive either carnations or tulips.

5. Ms. Olstad and the one who lives in Wisconsin both used to live next door to Judy; Jane used to live on the other side of town.

6. Neither Trudy, who never lived next door to Judy, nor Sharon received the basket of daisies.

7. Ms. Lansing moved away before Sharon.

The solution is on page 139.

The solution is on page 139.

first name				
last name				
flower				
state				

16 PAR FOR THE COURSE

by Ellen K. Rodehorst

After finishing a round of golf, Sherrie and her three friends went to the clubhouse to relax and tally their scores. On the last hole, all the women, who included Ms. Green, had different scores. Each of the four has a different color golf bag; one is black. From the information below, can you discover each woman's full name, the color of her bag, and her score on the last hole?

1. The golfer who shot one under par on the last hole is not the owner of the gold bag.

2. Ms. White, whose bag isn't white, is not the one who took six strokes to finish the last hole.

3. Ms. Gold, who is not Helen and doesn't own the gold bag, shot par on the last hole.

4. Judy, who is not Ms. Black, isn't the owner of the white bag.

5. Ms. Black, who isn't the owner of the gold bag, took three more strokes than Helen to finish the last hole.

6. Neither Beth nor the golfer with the green bag liked her score; both shot over par on the last hole, one scoring five strokes.

The solution is on page 139.

Score	First Name	Last Name	Bag Color
_____	_____	_____	_____
_____	_____	_____	_____
_____	_____	_____	_____
_____	_____	_____	_____

17 LAST-MINUTE SHOPPERS

by Julie Spence

Roy and Diana were among the last five customers waited on at Duren's store last Saturday. Each purchased one last-minute item; one bought light bulbs. From the clues below, can you determine the full names of these customers, what each purchased, and the order in which they were waited on?

1. The first customer waited on was not Woodbury.

2. Marge was waited on before Clark.

3. Joan was waited on after the woman who bought tape and before Mr. Barker.

4. Harold was waited on just after the customer who bought flash cubes and before Frye, who is not the one who bought ribbon.

5. Mr. Schiller was not the man who bought batteries.

The solution is on page 140.

	Customer		Purchase
1	_____	_____	_____
2	_____	_____	_____
3	_____	_____	_____
4	_____	_____	_____
5	_____	_____	_____

18 CONDO COMPLEX

by Cheryl L. McLaughlin

Cathy and her husband live in a six-story condominium on East Avenue. From the clues, can you determine the full names of all six couples living in the building (one surname is Brooks) and which floor each couple occupies?

1. Dave Ellis and his wife live one floor below Irma and one floor above the Kanes.

2. Ann lives on a lower floor than do Donna and her husband, Frank and his wife, and a third couple, but on a higher floor than the Manns or Mary and her husband John.

3. Henry lives two floors above Mr. Kane, who lives two floors above the Hills.

4. Sue and Mike live one floor below Bob, who lives three floors below the Gordons.

The solution is on page 140.

47

19 BARBERSHOP QUARTET

by Randall L. Whipkey

Not only do the four members of the Summerset Barbershop Quartet always win awards at singing, but each is also an expert stylist at a different local shop, one working at Bob's Barbershop. Given the clues below, can you find each member's full name, his voice part in the quartet, and the local establishment for which he cuts hair?

1. The four members of the Summerset Barbershop Quartet are Jack, Wilson, the stylist at the Hair Hut, and one of the two tenors.

2. Dailey isn't the group's baritone.

3. The barber at Daring-Do's isn't the quartet's bass.

4. The one who works at the Hair Hut, who isn't Graham, doesn't sing bass.

5. Graham isn't the Daring-Do's stylist.

6. Neither Tom nor Meyers sings tenor.

7. The bass isn't Wilson.

8. Ray and the Comb & Co. stylist are both Summerset School of Styling grads.

9. Bill and Graham work at different shops at Summerset Mall.

The solution is on page 140.

	Dailey	Graham	Meyers	Wilson	Bob's	Comb	Daring	Hair	Bar.	Bass	Ten.	Ten.
Bill												
Jack												
Ray												
Tom												
Bar.												
Bass												
Tenor												
Tenor												
Bob's												
Comb												
Daring												
Hair												

20 HOME-CARE WORKSHOP

by Diane C. Baldwin

George and three of his neighbors were among those who signed up for the home-care workshops sponsored by the local extension service. Four different classes were offered at three separate times during the day. Each chose three of the four classes, all in different combinations. One of the classes taught kitchen remodeling. Using the information below, can you list the classes, in order, that each person attended?

1. Larry and Nina attended their first and third classes together.

2. None of the four attended the lawn-care class at the same time.

3. Neither man went to both the insulation class and the wallpapering class.

4. Nina and one of the men took their second class together.

5. Larry and Bette both attended the lawn-care and wallpapering classes, but neither took them last.

The solution is on page 140.

CLASSES

insulation	kitchen	lawn	wallpaper
_____	_____	_____	_____
_____	_____	_____	_____
_____	_____	_____	_____

Bette   _____ _____ _____

George   _____ _____ _____

Larry   _____ _____ _____

Nina   _____ _____ _____

49

21 HOLIDAY CARDS

by Diane C. Baldwin

One day in December, the Burbanks received holiday cards from the Warrens and four other married couples, each old friends from different states. From the clues given, can you match the first and last names signed on each card (one husband is Bill) with the state, and tell the order in which the cards were opened?

1. Linda and Carol (whose husbands have the same first initial) sent, in some order, the last two cards to be opened.

2. The card from Pennsylvania wasn't from Carol and her husband.

3. The card from Joe and his wife was opened just before the one from Sue and her husband and just after the one from Massachusetts, which wasn't from the Dales.

4. The fourth card, which was not from Bruce, was not from the Browns; Sandy is not Mrs. Brown.

5. The card from Illinois was opened just before the one from Bob and his wife and just after the card from the Martins.

6. The Nye card was opened just after the one from John and his wife and just before the one from Delaware.

7. The husband's first name on the third card begins with "B."

8. Lucia and her husband live in Vermont.

The solution is on page 141.

	Husband	Wife	Last Name	State
1				
2				
3				
4				
5				

22 PICNIC IN THE PARK

by Mary A. Powell

On May 31, three generations of the Flowers family traipsed to the park to enjoy a picnic. The picnickers come from three separate households, each of which has a dog. From the following clues, can you find the name of the dog plus the full names and ages of the members in each household? (All members of a household share the same last name.)

1. Each woman had two daughters with her at the picnic.

2. These three live in different homes—Lily, the dog named Daisy, and Mrs. Meadows.

3. Jasmine and her cousin Daphne are both 12.

4. Violet is three years younger than her sister, Rose is two years younger than her sister, and Iris is one year younger than her sister.

5. The dog named Petunia lives with a woman who is 34.

6. The dog named Pansy does not live with either Jasmine or the 10-year-old.

7. Mrs. Field is 20 years younger than Mrs. Flowers.

8. Myrtle is an only child.

9. No one in the family is 11 or 33.

The solution is on page 141.

Use this space for solving.

by W. H. Organ

The Hillcrest Tennis Club, which this year is hosting the annual tennis match against its long-time rival the Village Country Club, has four members on its team who are playing against Village for the first time, and the Village Club has three players who have never before played against Hillcrest. From the following clues, can you determine the full names of each club's new players (one first name is Anita, and one surname is Lopez) and the event in which each is scheduled to play?

1. One of the new players is entered in the men's singles, one in the women's singles, and one in the men's doubles; the other four new players are two pairs who will be opponents in the mixed doubles.

2. Dick Hutton is playing in a doubles match.

3. John's partner in this year's match was a loser in last year's games between the two clubs.

4. Jim Kent and Kate, who is not Spencer, play for the same club.

5. Ms. Marble and Carl play for different clubs.

6. Tilden is not entered in the mixed doubles.

7. Carl's partner is Spencer.

8. Mary Hill is not entered in the women's singles.

The solution is on page 141.

Event	Name		Club

24 HOME-TOWN REUNION

by Mary A. Powell

Mrs. Martin and four other women who grew up together in a small town in Indiana have met for a long weekend every three years since their college days. Some have moved to other states; one lives in California, another in Pennsylvania. This year, the gathering will be in their home town. From the following clues, can you find each woman's full name (one first name is Judy), maiden name, present residence, and profession? NOTE: All the women are married, and all have adopted their husband's surnames.

1. At the first reunion, Ellen and the former Miss Bates married the Johnson brothers in a double-ring ceremony; the third reunion was in Oregon at the home of one of the two teachers; the fifth was at Sue's home; and this year's will be hosted by the department-store buyer. (Note: All five women are mentioned here.)

2. Cheryl, who is at least two years older than the other four, and the Realtor are sisters who both live on the West Coast.

3. Mrs. Owens and one of the Sanders girls are the same age.

4. Kay and the former Miss Engel have no brothers-in-law.

5. Mrs. Parker, who is not the one whose maiden name was Davis, is not a teacher.

6. The computer programmer is not the woman who lives in Maryland.

The solution is on page 142.

First Name	Maiden Name	Married Name	Occupation	State

25   BATON TWIRLERS' UNIFORMS

by Margaret Shoop

The members of Omni High School's marching band wear red-white-and-blue uniforms. Recently, when new uniforms were to be purchased for the band's six identically-dressed baton twirlers, it was decided that they would wear hats of one color, blouses of a second color, and skirts of the third color. But which should be what color? Fran and the other five twirlers were asked to vote. Unfortunately, no two twirlers came up with the same scheme (for example, only one twirler wanted the hats to be red, the blouses white, and the skirts blue), so the band director had to make the final decision. From the clues below, determine how each twirler voted.

1. Amanda's and Cassie's blouse-color preferences were the same, and matched Beverly's and Dot's skirt-color preferences.

2. Amanda voted for red hats; Beverly did not vote for red blouses.

3. The color that Cassie wanted for the hats was not the same as the color that Elaine wanted for the blouses.

4. Cassie's color choice for the hats was not blue.

The solution is on page 142.

1.

2.

3.

4.

5.

6.

26 CHARITY DRIVE

by Cheryl L. McLaughlin

Art and four others headed the five fund-raising committees in Oakdale's recent charity drive, representing Oakdale's boys' club, girls' club, day care center, senior center, and park district. All the committees raised different amounts of money from $500 to $2500. Each committee sought funds for a different purpose; one wanted to purchase art equipment. From the following clues, can you determine each committee head's full name (one surname is Oger), the amount each raised, and its purpose?

1. Mr. Quinn's committee raised $1000 more than Flora's, which wasn't the seniors' committee; the committee that sought funds for a day camp raised $1000 more than the boys' club committee.

2. Neither Ellie, who headed the girls' club committee, nor Reed was on the committee seeking funds for the activity center.

3. Jerry's committee, which sought funds for kitchen equipment, raised $500 less than Darla's day care center committee but $500 more than Mr. Nagler's committee.

4. One committee raised $1500 for bus service.

5. Pace didn't head the park district committee.

The solution is on page 143.

Note: Spaces for some amounts raised have been left empty for you to fill in when you determine them.

	N	O	P	Q	R	boys'	girls'	day	sen.	park	act.	art	bus	camp	kit.	500				2500
Art																				
Darla																				
Ellie																				
Flora																				
Jerry																				
500																				
2500																				
act.																				
art																				
bus																				
camp																				
kit.																				
boys'																				
girls'																				
day																				
sen.																				
park																				

27 FIVE GOLD RINGS

by Diane Yoko

To aid in the cost of buying new gymnastic equipment for Sunrise Valley High, a white elephant sale was conducted. June and four other women donated gold rings, all different whole sizes and containing different stones (one had a sapphire). From the following clues, can you determine each woman's full name (one surname is Bremer) and the size and stone of the gold ring she donated?

1. The jade ring was the smallest, two sizes smaller than the ring Babs donated (which wasn't the ruby).

2. The topaz ring was not the largest size.

3. The ring Mandell donated, which wasn't the emerald, was four sizes smaller than the one donated by Ruth.

4. The ring Tucker donated was one size larger than the one Anna donated and three sizes larger than the ruby ring, which was size five.

5. The emerald ring was smaller than the ring Jacobs donated.

6. Toni, who isn't Warley, donated neither the smallest nor the largest size ring.

The solution is on page 143.

	Bremer	Jacobs	Mandell	Tucker	Warley	emerald	jade	ruby	sapphire	topaz	size				
Anna															
Babs															
June															
Ruth															
Toni															

size							emerald	jade	ruby	sapphire	topaz

	Bremer	Jacobs	Mandell	Tucker	Warley
emerald					
jade					
ruby					
sapphire					
topaz					

28 THE TUTORS

by Margaret Shoop

Felton and five other people operate a business that offers tutoring in six high-school subject areas. Each of the six instructs in two subjects, and each subject is handled by two of the six. From the clues that follow, can you determine each tutor's subjects?

1. Evans does not teach English.

2. Adams does not teach French.

3. Vine teaches French.

4. Dalton tutors in neither English nor physics.

5. Corelli's subjects are math and physics.

6. One of the tutors in chemistry is Evans.

7. The one who teaches English and French isn't Vine.

8. Neither Dalton nor Evans tutors in history.

The solution is on page 143.

TUTORS

Adams _____ _____

Corelli _____ _____

Dalton _____ _____

Evans _____ _____

Felton _____ _____

Vine _____ _____

SUBJECTS

chem. _____ _____

Eng. _____ _____

Fr. _____ _____

hist. _____ _____

math _____ _____

physics _____ _____

29 UP, UP, AND AWAY!

by Mary Marks Cezus

Fred and three of his friends participated in Baldwin's Balloon Bust this past weekend. Each of their hot air balloons is a different color and won the first place award in a different category. Using the clues below, can you determine each person's full name, balloon color, and category in which the balloon won?

1. A photographer from the Baldwin Press asked three of the winners—Denise, the person who won the greatest speed category, and the person who owns the purple balloon—to pose for a picture together.

2. Flynn, the person who owns the red balloon, and the person who won the creativity of design award all met for dinner Friday evening.

3. Craig (who does not own the blue balloon) and Highland (who does not own the gold balloon) once shared ownership in a balloon.

4. Denise (who is not Adair) and the person who won the beauty of design category both participated in the Baldwin Balloon Bust last year.

5. Upton (who does not own the red balloon) and the person who won the longest distance category were both interviewed by WFLY.

6. The person who won the creativity of design category (who is not Upton) and the owner of the purple balloon plan to collaborate on a book about hot air balloons.

7. The person who owns the gold balloon, Adair (who is not Ellen), and the person who won the greatest speed category all live in different states.

The solution is on page 144.

	Adair	Flynn	Highland	Upton	beauty	creat.	dis.	speed	blue	gold	purple	red
Craig												
Denise												
Ellen												
Fred												
blue												
gold												
purple												
red												
beauty												
creat.												
dis.												
speed												

30 1950s FANTASY FILM FESTIVAL

by Susan Zivich

The Old Town Theater celebrated the Fabulous Fifties with a February Fantasy Film Festival. For three weeks, they offered a double bill of classics from that decade. From the following clues, can you determine the two movies shown each week as well as each film's director, male and female leads, and the year it was released? And pass the popcorn, please.

1. "Enchanted Island" was directed by Allan Dwan.

2. "Safari" and the movie made in 1958 were featured the first week.

3. "Son of Ali Baba" was made in 1952, while the movie directed by Richard Thorpe was filmed in 1951.

4. The movie with Janet Leigh, which was filmed in 1956, was shown the week before "Ivanhoe."

5. Terence Young directed the movie with Victor Mature.

6. Dana Andrews and Jane Powell appeared in the same movie.

7. The final week brought "Solomon and Sheba" and the movie starring Piper Laurie. One of them was directed by Kurt Neumann.

8. Elizabeth Taylor starred in "Ivanhoe" and Stewart Granger starred in "Salome."

9. The movie with Rita Hayworth was filmed in 1953.

10. King Vidor directed Gina Lollobrigida in the movie that ran the same week as the one starring Tony Curtis.

11. The movies featured the second week were the one that was directed by William Dieterle and the one starring Robert Taylor.

12. Yul Brynner starred in the movie filmed in 1959, but did not share top billing with Elizabeth Taylor.

The solution is on page 144.

WEEK 1

_____ _____ and _____ _____

Starring in (year) _____ _____

Directed by _____

*****************************PLUS*****************************

_____ _____ and _____ _____

Starring in (year) _____ _____

Directed by _____

WEEK 2

_____ _____ and _____ _____

Starring in (year) _____ _____

Directed by _____

*****************************PLUS*****************************

_____ _____ and _____ _____

Starring in (year) _____ _____

Directed by _____

WEEK 3

_____ _____ and _____ _____

Starring in (year) _____ _____

Directed by _____

*****************************PLUS*****************************

_____ _____ and _____ _____

Starring in (year) _____ _____

Directed by _____

31 JAMES BOMB, AGENT 000

by Randall L. Whipkey

The most successful movie sequels of all time are the James Bomb, Agent 000, films. Sixteen Bomb movies have been made, starring five different actors. From these clues, can you uncover the order in which the five have been Bomb, the first James Bomb film each made, and the number of Bomb movies in which he has starred?

1. Roger Bore has made more James Bomb films than Sean Corny and the actor who first played Bomb in "Doctor Yes" have made together.

2. The actor who first played Bomb in "Brassfinger" immediately preceded and made one more Agent 000 movie than Timothy Dullthing.

3. David Never isn't the one who debuted in "You Only Live Thrice."

4. The fourth James Bomb made twice as many Bomb films as the second James Bomb.

5. The first James Bomb made the most Agent 000 films, twice as many as the actor who first played the spy in "Zircons Are Forever."

6. George Lazyboy immediately preceded the "Brassfinger" star in the series.

7. Roger Bore isn't the one who first starred in "From Bulgaria With Love" or the actor who made his Bomb debut in "You Only Live Thrice."

8. Timothy Dullthing's initial Bomb appearance wasn't in "Doctor Yes."

9. Each of the actors has starred in a different number of films.

The solution is on page 144.

	Brass	Bulgaria	Dr. Yes	Thrice	Zircons	1st	2nd	3rd	4th	5th	number of movies				
Roger Bore															
Sean Corny															
Tim Dullthing															
George Lazyboy															
David Never															
# of movies															
1st															
2nd															
3rd															
4th															
5th															

62

32 RECREATIONAL SPORTS

by Fred H. Dale

Jane and four of her friends enjoy different recreation sports, one of which is tennis. The group ranges in age from twelve to eighteen, with no two the same age. From the following clues, you should be able to tell the age and favorite sport of each of the five.

1. Bill is as much older than the golfer as he is younger than Mary.

2. The bowler is as much older than the hiker as John is older than Bill. (Note: Do not assume four different people are mentioned in this clue.)

3. Tom is a year younger than Mary, and a year older than the hiker.

4. The swimmer is older than the bowler.

The solution is on page 145.

Use this space for solving.

33 CHINESE ZODIAC

by W. H. Organ

Miss Wong and two other members of the Chinese Women's Swim Team were enjoying tea with three members of the visiting U.S. Women's Swim Team. All of them were entered in different events (one was the 200 yd. race). During their conversation, they learned they were all born in different cities and in different years of the Chinese zodiac. (One was the Year of the Dog). From the following clues can you determine their full names, swim events, birthplaces, (one was Shanghai), and the Chinese zodiac years in which they were born?

1. The girl who is entered in the 100 yd. event and the one who was born in the Year of the Rat are entered in an international swim meet for the first time.

2. Mei Lin, who was born in Honolulu, and the Smith girl, whose event is the backstroke, have both competed once before.

3. Rose, who was born in Denver, and Min Chi, who was born in the Year of the Sheep, have competed in several meets.

4. Lee's event was the 50 yd. race. She was not born in Peking.

5. Sally's event is not the 100 yd. distance. She was born in Boston in the Year of the Monkey.

6. Mary was born in Hong Kong in the Year of the Boar.

7. The Jones girl, who is competing for the first time, was not born in the Year of the Rat.

8. The Kent girl's event is diving. She was born in the Year of the Horse.

9. Mei Lin's event was not the breast stroke.

Editor's note: Do not assume that Oriental names and/or birthplaces automatically go together.

The solution is on page 145.

Because of the size of this chart, it had to be divided in two, but it is used in the normal way for solving.

	Chi	Jones	Kent	Lin	Smith	Wong	Bos.	Den.	H.K.	Hono.	Pek.	Shang.	50 yd.	100 yd.	200 yd.	back.	brst.	dive
Lee																		
Mary																		
Mei																		
Min																		
Rose																		
Sally																		
Boar																		
Dog																		
Horse																		
Monkey																		
Rat																		
Sheep																		
50 yd.																		
100 yd.																		
200 yd.																		
back.																		
brst.																		
dive																		
Bos.																		
Den.																		
H.K.																		
Hono.																		
Pek.																		
Shang.																		

	Boar	Dog	Horse	Monkey	Rat	Sheep
Lee						
Mary						
Mei						
Min						
Rose						
Sally						

34 TELEPHONE LISTINGS

by Margaret Shoop

Dover City's telephone directory has an alphabetical section for business listings called the "green pages." In it, the names Finnegan, Finneran, Fione, Fiore, and Firster appear as five consecutive listings. Each listing includes a set of initials (including M.N.), an indication of the business each is in (one specifies insurance), and a telephone number, all of which have different exchanges (one is 274). From the clues that follow, can you deduce the full name, type of business, and telephone exchange of each listing?

1. The listing with the 272 exchange comes sometime after the listing with the initials F.J. and just before the orthodontist's listing.

2. The five listings are: Fione's, the minister's, the one with the initials T.U., Fiore's, and the one in advertising.

3. The listing with the initials R.H. is above the minister's listing.

4. Fione, who is not the physician, is the one whose telephone number begins with 271; the listing with the 275 exchange comes just before the physician's listing (which isn't Firster's).

5. The initials K.L. do not appear in either the 271 or the 273 exchange, nor are they in the minister's listing.

The solution is on page 146.

Finnegan, _____ _____ #_____
Finneran, _____ _____ #_____
Fione,   _____ _____ #_____
Fiore,   _____ _____ #_____
Firster, _____ _____ #_____

	FJ	KL	MN	RH	TU	advert.	ins.	min.	ortho.	phys.	271	272	273	274	275
Finnegan															
Finneran															
Fione															
Fiore															
Firster															
271															
272															
273															
274															
275															
advert.															
ins.															
min.															
ortho.															
phys.															

35 THE TALLER, THE HEAVIER?

by Evelyn B. Rosenthal

Two statisticians at a certain university agree that there is a high correlation between height and weight, but differ about the likelihood of finding exceptions. One said that if four men were taken at random, their rankings in order of height and weight would be the same; the other doubted this. They agreed to test the hypothesis by picking four students. From the following clues, can you find each student's full name (one first name is Jeff, one surname Stone), major, height, and weight?

1. There is a difference of exactly two inches between each height and a difference of exactly twenty pounds between each weight.

2. The first statistician was wrong in at least one instance; the student who weighs 170 pounds is shorter than the one who weighs 150 pounds.

3. The French major is heavier than Eric and lighter than the English major.

4. Peck is the heaviest; the chemistry major the lightest.

5. Gary is taller than at least one of the others, but shorter than the English major.

6. The math major is taller than Harry and shorter than Finn.

7. Eric, who is not Vogel, is not the lightest.

8. The number of pounds of the lightest is twice the number of inches of the shortest, who is between five and six feet tall.

The solution is on page 146.

	Finn	Peck	Stone	Vogel	chem.	Eng.	Fr.	math
Eric								
Gary								
Harry								
Jeff								
chem.								
Eng.								
Fr.								
math								

WEIGHT

___ _____ _____ ___
___ _____ _____ ___
___ _____ _____ ___
___ _____ _____ ___

HEIGHT

___ _____ _____ ___
___ _____ _____ ___
___ _____ _____ ___
___ _____ _____ ___

36 BALANCING SEESAWS

by Anne Smith

One afternoon, eight children went to their neighborhood park to play on the three seesaws. Luckily, the children chose seats on the seesaws so that each seesaw was in balance. From the following clues, determine each child's full name (two first names were Jim and Joy, and one surname was Jones) and weight, as well as who shared seesaws.

1. All weights were in whole numbers of pounds.

2. On one seesaw, Jane sat by herself on one side while the Jefferson boy and the girl who weighed 45 pounds sat together on the other side.

3. The other two seesaws were shared by the Johnson twins (who both weighed 60 pounds and were the only two to weigh the same), the Jackson brothers, and Jenny's brother (who was the lightest one on his seesaw).

4. Joe weighed twice as much as Jenny; the Jenkins girl weighed twice as much as John.

5. Jeff weighed 10 pounds less than Janis.

6. No child weighed more than 100 pounds.

The solution is on page 146.

68

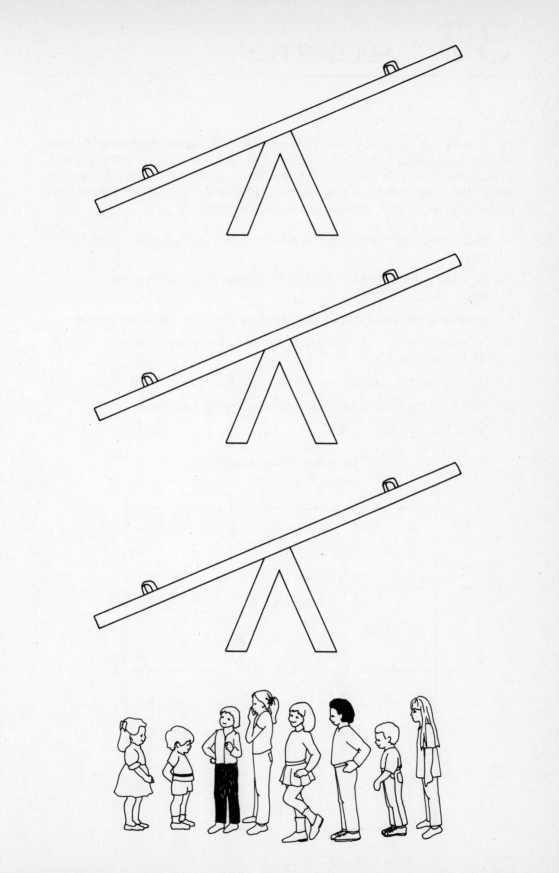

37   SPECIALTIES

by Ellen K. Rodehorst

Dr. Spencer and three other physicians opened offices on the third floor of a new medical building. All four doctors, including Richard, specialize in a different area of medicine (one is an allergist). The third floor has four identical offices, each facing the central elevator. From the information below, can you determine each doctor's full name, medical speciality, and office number?

1. The pediatrician, who's office is next to Ann's, did not choose 330 for his office.

2. Dr. Cline's office, which isn't 320, is diagonally across from the surgeon's office.

3. Dr. Miller's office and office 330 are both on the north side of the building.

4. The internist, who isn't John, chose the office that is next to both Dr. Winter's office and office 310.

5. Margaret's office, which is not 330, is on the west side of the building.

6. Ann chose the office in the southeast corner of the building.

7. Office 310 is not next to 340.

The solution is on page 147.

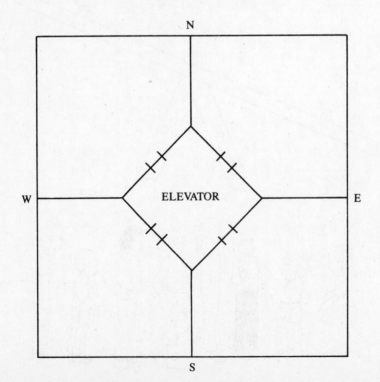

70

38 BUSY MORNING

by Evelyn B. Rosenthal

Ms. Hanks and five other women, who all live on different floors of a 22-story apartment building, were very busy one recent Saturday morning. All wanted to do the same four chores; however, each succeeded in accomplishing only three of them, and no two did the same three in the same order. From the following clues, can you find each woman's full name (one first name is Mary), her floor, and which chores she did in what order that morning?

1. Cleaning house was done by all six, either first or last.

2. The woman whose floor number is twice Flo's and half Ms. Nelson's, the highest, went to the library first.

3. The women who washed their hair did it last of their three chores.

4. The lowest floor any of the six lives on is the fourth, and none lives on the fifth or the twelfth floor.

5. The women who live on the lowest two of the three consecutive floors among the six didn't do the same three chores as each other or as anyone else.

6. The woman on the second-highest floor went to the bank first; her floor number is the sum of those of Connie and Ms. Briggs.

7. Joan's floor number is twice that of a woman who washed her hair; both did the same chore second that morning.

8. The woman whose floor is as far from Ann's as Ann's is from Ms. Kraft's went to the library last.

9. The woman who lives on the highest floor of the six went to the bank last.

10. Grace Elmont lives on a lower floor than Ms. Duncan.

The solution is on page 147.

Floor	First Name	Last Name	Chores		

by Susan Zivich

Heritage Mall merchants celebrated the town's Founders' Day by handing out small gifts to their customers. From the following clues, can you determine the location of each store, each store's owner (one is Mr. Meyer), and what item was given away?

1. The four stores on the lower level are: the clothes store, the store that passed out seed packets, and the two stores owned by Mr. Fleming and Mr. Chadwick.

2. The fabric shop is not the one owned by Ms. Jacobson.

3. The four stores on the south side of the mall are: the record store, the pet store, the store owned by Ms. Nicholas, and the store that offered pocket calendars to customers.

4. The store that offered lapel pins was directly under the card shop.

5. The four stores on the north side of the mall are: the shoe store, Ms. Gallagher's store, and the stores that offered the ruler and the refrigerator magnet.

6. The four stores on the upper level are: the pet store, the store that passed out memo pads, and the stores owned by Ms. Duncan and Ms. Jacobson.

7. The store that passed out keychains is directly under Ms. Gallagher's store.

8. The four stores on the east side of the mall are: the toy store, Mr. Westcott's store, and the two stores that passed out a refrigerator magnet and a balloon.

9. The four stores on the west side of the mall are: the book store, the card shop, Mr. Chadwick's store, and the store that gave customers a keychain.

The solution is on page 148.

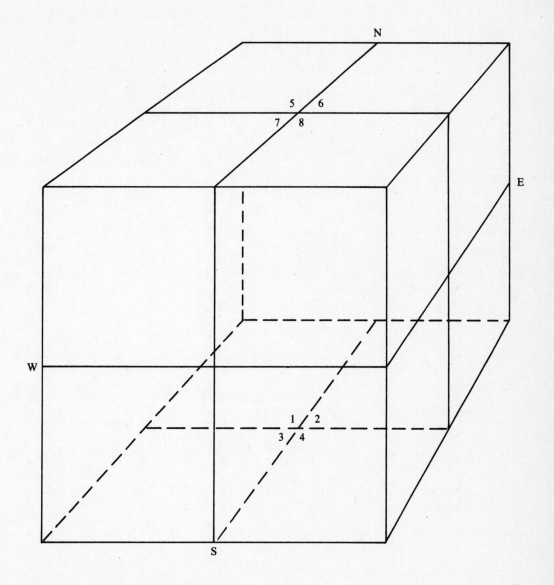

HARD LOGIC PROBLEMS

40 DOUGHNUTS

by Mary A. Powell

Friday morning is doughnut day in the sales department of Acme Products, and Lila and four other employees have placed the same order every Friday for the last two years. Last week, however, each ordered something different. From the following clues, can you find the full names of the five employees, how each took his or her coffee and the pastry each ordered last week (including one apple fritter), and the pastry each usually orders (including a maple bar)?

1. Two employees always order black coffee with no sugar; the other three are Jeremy, the one who usually orders a bear claw, and the one who ordered a bran muffin last week.

2. Roger, Workman, and the person who usually orders the cheese Danish take cream and/or sugar in their coffee.

3. Carol is neither the employee who usually orders the raspberry Danish nor the one who ordered the prune Danish last week.

4. Neither Bert nor Fuller is the employee who ordered the blueberry muffin last week.

5. Both Quiller and the employee who ordered the cinnamon roll last week take cream in their coffee.

6. Cox and the one who usually orders the cinnamon twist take sugar in their coffee.

7. Parker has never ordered a Danish.

8. Jeremy does not use sugar in his coffee.

The solution is on page 148.

First Name	Last Name	Coffee Order	Usual Order	Last Week

41 THE COLTS

by Margaret Shoop

A famous jumping stable boasts six thoroughbred colts of distinguished breeding, including Mercury's Boy and Quicksilver. The six are the offspring of four mares, including Hob Nob. From the clues which follow, can you determine the names of each colt's dam (mother) and sire (father)?

1. The three stallions—Commendation, Dooby Do, and Spectacular—each sired two colts.

2. The two colts named Go For It and High Falutin have the same sire.

3. None of the four mares is the mother of more than two of the six colts.

4. The two colts named High Falutin and Lucky Fellow are related.

5. The two colts named Catch Me Now and Lucky Fellow are related; neither is the offspring of Commendation.

6. One or more of the colts is the offspring of Spectacular and the mare named Fabulous.

7. Two of the colts are the offspring of Dooby Do and the mare named Clockbreaker.

8. Go For It is not the offspring of Commendation and the mare named Heights of Glory, but at least one of the colts is their offspring.

The solution is on page 149.

Colt	Dam	Sire

42 NEW SUITS

by Diane Yoko

Brant, Landman, and four other men purchased suits yesterday at Manny's Men's Clothing. From the following clues, can you deduce the full names of the six men, the color and price of the suit each bought, and place their purchases in the order they were bought?

1. Anthony did not buy the brown suit.

2. The brown suit was purchased earlier in the day than either of the green ones.

3. Larry's purchase immediately followed Carter's.

4. David's suit cost $100 more than the last one purchased.

5. Miller's purchase, which wasn't the last, was made just after Anthony's, which was made immediately after the gray suit was bought.

6. Matt's suit cost $50 less than Donovan's.

7. The navy suit was the same price as one of the others.

8. A green suit was purchased just before Charles bought his suit; Donovan's purchase was next after Charles's and was immediately followed by the purchase of a suit that cost $150.

9. Charles bought neither the black nor the gray suit.

10. None of the men has the same first and last initials.

11. Larry's suit cost twice as much as Akins'; Akins bought neither a green nor a black suit.

12. Burt's suit cost twice as much as Charles's.

The solution is on page 149.

	Akins	Brant	Carter	Donovan	Landman	Miller
Anthony						
Burt						
Charles						
David						
Larry						
Matt						

#	first name	last name	color	price
1				
2				
3				
4				
5				
6				

43 SWEET MIX

by Mary Marks Cezus

Walter and five friends recently purchased a selection of candies together. Each person chose exactly one kind of candy. No two people chose the same kind or the same number of candies. Using the clues below can you determine each person's first name, last name (one was Wolfe), kind of candy, and number of candies (5, 6, 8, 10, 13, or 16)?

1. The person who chose the vanilla nuggets chose more than twice as many candies as Heidi (who did not select the raspberry rolls).

2. The person whose last name is Sullivan picked out more than Darren but fewer than the number of fudge fingers.

3. The person who chose the cinnamon squares chose more candies than Becky (who did not choose the butter ribbons).

4. Louise chose more candies than the person whose last name is Montgomery but fewer than the person who chose the choco-caramels.

5. The person who chose the butter ribbons (which were not chosen by Heidi) and the person whose last name is Coleman both had a difficult time choosing only one kind of candy.

6. Tom is not Sullivan.

7. Montgomery chose more candies than the person whose last name is Hines.

8. The person whose last name is Farley (who is not Louise) and the person who chose the fudge fingers both enjoy trying out candy recipes.

The solution is on page 150.

	Coleman	Farley	Hines	Mont.	Sull.	Wolfe	butter ribbon	choco cara.	cin. sq.	fudge fing.	rasp. roll	van. nug.	# OF PIECES					
Becky																		
Darren																		
Heidi																		
Louise																		
Tom																		
Walter																		
but. rib.																		
choco.-car.																		
cin. sq.																		
fudge fing.																		
rasp. roll																		
van. nug.																		

80

44 HOW MANY CANDLES?

by Diane Yoko

Each of the six children at a birthday party, including the birthday child, wore a different color hat. From the following clues, can you determine each child's full name (one last name is Cummings), hat color, and age, as well as whose birthday it was and how many candles were on the cake? (*Note:* Don't forget to add one candle for good luck!)

1. Chuck and Lynn are the only children who are an odd number of years old.

2. The Foster child, who isn't Lynn, is one year older than the child who wore the pink hat.

3. The Baker child is the same age as Adam.

4. The Ramsey child is ten years old, one year younger than the child who wore the blue hat and two years older than Jill.

5. The Harris child, who isn't Cindy, and the March child are the same age.

6. Randy is one year older than the child who wore the green hat.

7. The nine-year-old child is not Lynn.

8. Adam's hat was not the yellow one.

9. Cindy and the child who wore the purple hat are the same age.

10. The birthday child wore the orange hat.

The solution is on page 150.

	Baker	Cummings	Foster	Harris	March	Ramsey	blue	green	orange	pink	purple	yellow	ages					
Adam																		
Chuck																			
Cindy																			
Jill																			
Lynn																			
Randy																			

ages												
blue						
green						
orange						
pink						
purple						
yellow						

45 BARGAIN BONANZA

by Cheryl L. McLaughlin

Sam, Lisa, and four others each bought an item at a neighborhood yard sale; each also sold one item to one of the other five. From the clues, can you determine each person's full name (one surname is Cox), what each bought and sold, and each item's price?

1. The one who bought the crib sold the bike for $25.

2. Jason, who sold a set of tires for $60, isn't O'Keefe, who bought the radio.

3. Ms. Heston bought tires and sold a $40 item to Dixie, who isn't Firth.

4. Bellamy sold a dryer for $50 to Ava, who spent $30 more than she made.

5. Dan sold the TV to Reid, who ended up $15 richer.

The solution is on page 150.

First Name					
Last Name					
Bought					
Sold					

46 DIET DELIGHTS

by Susan Zivich

Janet and five fellow members of the Diet Delights Club recently lost a total of 70 pounds; no two lost the same amount. From the following clues, can you find each woman's full name (one surname is Martin), occupation, and weight loss?

1. Mary, who lost the most weight, lost eight pounds more than the accountant.

2. Ms. Johnson lost five pounds more than Nancy.

3. Trudy is a photographer.

4. Either Anne lost twelve pounds and the lawyer eighteen or vice versa.

5. Ms. Andrews lost the least, seven pounds.

6. Ms. Stevens lost more weight than the musician.

7. Sarah's last name is Nelson.

8. The zoologist lost eight pounds.

9. Ms. Taylor lost five pounds more than the saleswoman.

The solution is on page 151.

	Andrews	Johnson	Martin	Nelson	Stevens	Taylor	acct	law	music	photo	sales	zoo	weight loss					
Anne																		
Janet																		
Mary																		
Nancy																		
Sarah																		
Trudy																		
weight loss																		
acct.																		
lawyer																		
music.																		
photo.																		
sales.																		
zoo.																		

47 FLOWERING TREES

by Evelyn B. Rosenthal

Laura and four other children in a nature study class were told to write the numerals 1 through 5 after the names of five trees to indicate the order in which they bloom. From the following clues, can you find the full name of each child (one surname is Andrews), and the numerals he or she assigned to each tree?

1. Mary thought the cherry was #5.

2. The Fox and Clark children didn't agree on the numerals for any tree.

3. The elm and the linden were both numbered correctly by three children and given the same incorrect numeral—one away from the right answer—by the other two.

4. Joe had most right answers; the only one of the others with the correct numeral for the horse-chestnut was next; then came Ellen; then the only one besides Joe who had the cherry right; and last, the Gregg child.

5. Mary and the Clark child gave the horse-chestnut the same numeral, as did Don and the Brown child; the other child said it was #1.

6. Joe gave the elm #1, the magnolia #2, the cherry #3, and the linden #5.

The solution is on page 151.

Use this space for solving.

48 AT THE AUCTION

by Cheryl L. McLaughlin

Five antique lovers, including one from Paris, each made one purchase at a recent auction; one item was a ruby ring. Each purchase cost a different whole number of dollars. From the following clues, can you determine each buyer's full name (one surname is Barrington), home city, purchase, and price of purchase?

1. The man from Beverly Hills paid twice as much for his jewelry as Maria, who is from London, paid for hers.

2. The oil painting cost $10,000 more than Graystone's purchase.

3. The silver tea service cost $5,000 less than Joseph's purchase, which cost $5,000 less than the item purchased by the man from Rome.

4. LaMar, who isn't Daniel, bought neither the diamond necklace nor the grandfather clock.

5. Jonathan's purchase was the least expensive.

6. Helena spent $15,000, which was more than the price of the clock although not the most expensive purchase.

7. Bandervilt paid twice as much as the person from New York, who isn't Vesterhouse.

The solution is on page 151.

First Name	Last Name	City	Purchase	Price

49 DESIGNER MUGS

by Mary Marks Cezus

Mullin's Muggery is featuring six designer mugs this month. They are hanging on display (as illustrated) with the mugs one, two, and three above mugs four, five, and six. No two mugs were designed by the same person nor do any two cost the same amount. Using the clues below, can you determine each mug's position, designer, name, and cost ($6, $7.50, $8, $8.50, $9.50, or $10)?

1. The mug designed by Ambrose (who did not design "Owl Family") is to the right of "Chipmunk Chase."

2. The mug designed by Giselle is to the right of "Scenic Farm" and is more expensive than the mug designed by Renata.

3. The mug designed by Florian is to the left of the least expensive mug and is below "Touchdown!"

4. "Owl Family" is above the mug designed by Brendan.

5. The mug designed by Renata is to the right of "Poppy Serenade" and is more expensive than "Chipmunk Chase."

6. "Owl Family" is more expensive than "Scenic Farm."

7. Neither Florian nor Zandra designed "Poppy Serenade."

8. Ambrose did not design "Butterfly Fantasy."

9. "Chipmunk Chase" is to the right of the mug designed by Renata and is more expensive than Brendan's, which is not the least expensive mug.

10. The mug designed by Florian costs more than "Butterfly Fantasy" but less than "Scenic Farm."

The solution is on page 152.

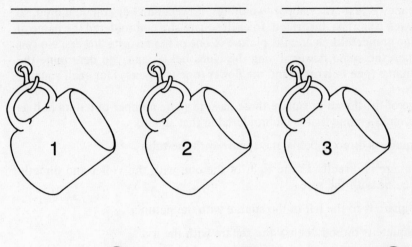

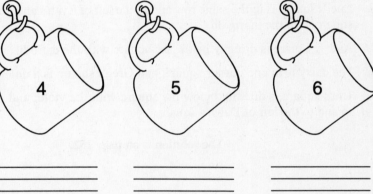

50   BLOOMIN' GRANDKIDS

by Mary Marks Cezus

Grandma Heaney is just crazy about two things, flowers and her grandchildren, so she made herself a shirt as illustrated. In each square she embroidered the name of one of her nine grandchildren and the picture of one of her favorite flowers. No two squares contain the same flower. Using the clues below, can you determine the grandchild's name (one is Kristy) and the flower (one is a pansy) for each square?

1. The name of the flower in square three has the same number of letters in it as the grandchild's name that is embroidered in that square.

2. Greg's square is directly below the square with the tulip.

3. Toby's square is directly to the right of the one with the violet and directly above the one with the rose.

4. Dawn's square is to the left of the square with the petunia.

5. Cindy's square is directly below the square with the iris.

6. Luci's square is in the same row and to the left of Ryan's and directly above the square with the marigold.

7. Andy's square is directly below the square with the daffodil.

8. The daisy is in one corner square, and Greg's square is a different corner.

9. Tim's square is directly below the square with the violet and in the same row as and to the left of Dawn's square.

The solution is on page 152.

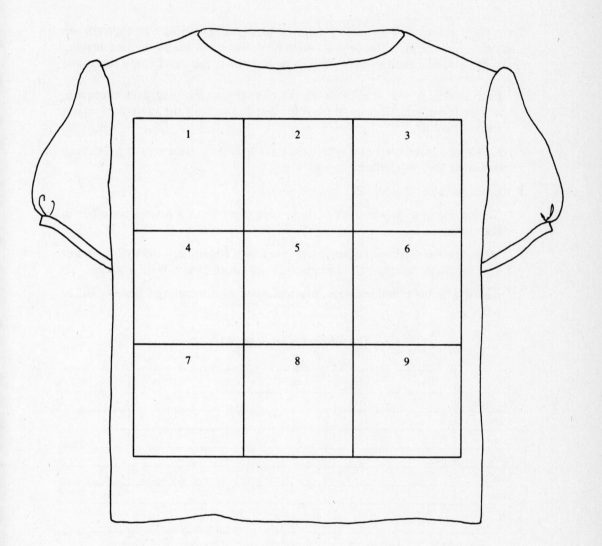

51 STUDENTS' SCHEDULES

by Mary A. Powell

Six college students, who attend daily classes and devote part of each day to studying, also have part-time jobs at which they work each day. From the following clues, can you find each student's full name and work, class and study schedule?

1. Each student works, studies, or attends classes each morning, each afternoon, and each evening, Monday through Friday; no two have the same work-class-study schedule.

2. Kathy and Price have two evening classes together; Price sees Ingalls every day since they work the same shift together.

3. Louis works in the political science library.

4. Collins and Nancy, who isn't Mason, work together at a newspaper office in the evenings.

5. Mark, who sometimes makes study dates with Christine, works while Baker studies; Steve, who has no afternoon classes, works while Walton studies.

6. Kathy, who never misses work, is a night owl who sometimes sleeps until 10 a.m.

The solution is on page 153.

	Baker	Collins	Ingalls	Mason	Price	Walton
Christine						
Kathy						
Louis						
Mark						
Nancy						
Steve						

First Name	Last Name	Morning	Afternoon	Evening

52 VALENTINE'S DAY PARTY

by Evelyn B. Rosenthal

When Mrs. Carlson picked up her daughter at kindergarten one Friday, she invited five of the child's friends to a Valentine's Day party the next day. Each of the six children, who included Barbara and Pat, picked a slip of paper with the name of one of the others on it and was asked to bring an inexpensive or homemade present for that child. From the following clues, can you find the full name of each child (one surname is Dobbs), the present he or she gave (one gift was a Valentine card, another a cupcake), its recipient, and its cost, if any?

1. The most expensive gift cost 30¢.

2. Each boy brought a gift for a girl; each girl brought a gift for a boy.

3. The paper flower was one of three homemade gifts.

4. The cost of the bag of peanuts was 10¢ less than the cost of the gift Mike brought and one-half the cost of the one he received.

5. No two children exchanged gifts with each other.

6. Lee, who drew the name of a child whose birthday fell on Valentine's Day, brought him a birthday card.

7. The least-expensive purchased gift was not the one received by the Burns child.

8. The Adams girl received her favorite brand of candy bar.

9. The Green child both gave and received a homemade gift.

10. The Ross child both gave and received something to eat.

11. Only Jane neither gave nor received something to eat.

12. The birthday boy, who is not Kit, did not bring peanuts.

The solution is on page 153.

Use this space for solving.

53 SEAT SWITCH

by Diane C. Baldwin

When John, Mark, and the other three boys in the first row of assigned seats heard they would have a substitute teacher, they decided to play a little trick by switching seats with one another. Using the clues below, can you identify each child by full name (two last names are Parker and Gallo) and his seat before and after the switch? *(All clues are from the students' perspective.)*

1. Mike moved over one seat farther than the Parton boy did.

2. The two boys with the same first and last initials had the end seats before the switch.

3. The Parton boy had the end seat next to Jerry after the switch.

4. Just two boys moved more than a seat away from their first seats.

5. Frank sat just to the left of the Penn boy before and after the switch.

6. The Bell boy moved three seats to his right.

The solution is on page 154.

BEFORE

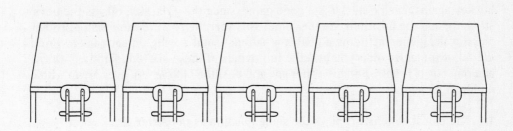

AFTER

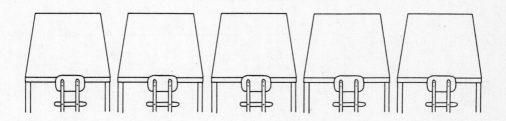

54   SOCKEY

by Evelyn B. Rosenthal

At the end of the fall sports season at our high school, the girls' field hockey team and the boys' soccer team celebrate with a "sockey" game, in which they play hockey against each other: it is a good game, since the girls' skill offsets the boys' strength, and the positions are the same. This year, there were three sister-brother pairs in the game, including a goalie, a halfback, and a wing on each team. From the following clues, can you find the full names of these six (one family is Burns and one boy is Frank), and his or her age and position? (*Note:* All ages are in whole numbers of years.)

1. The oldest, who is 17, plays the same position as the Adler girl.

2. Laura is one year older than her brother.

3. Mary is two years older than the Cox boy.

4. Nancy is the same age as one of the goalies.

5. The sister of the boy halfback plays the same position as the youngest, who is 14 years old.

6. The girl who plays wing is one year older than Dan.

7. The Adler twins are one year younger than Ed and one year older than the girl goalie.

The solution is on page 154.

The solution is on page 154.

	boy	girl
goalie		
halfback		
wing		

94

55 TV GAME SHOWS

by Randall L. Whipkey

Five good friends decided to apply to become contestants on various daytime television game shows, good-naturedly joking about who could win the most money. To their surprise, each got on the program of his or her choice and each won a different sum of money, the largest amount being $3,000. From the following clues, can you deduce which person was on each show and how much he or she won on the program?

1. Wes won four times as much as the contestant on *Kashword*.

2. The person on *Mr. Moneybags* won twice as much as Sue and four times as much as the contestant on *Greenback Bonanza*.

3. The contestant on *Pot O'Gold* won twice as much as Tex and three times as much as Vi.

4. Una won $1,000 more than the person on *Dollarama*.

The solution is on page 155.

Program	Contestant	Money

56 ICE-CREAM CONES

by Diane Yoko

At the Summer Day Feast Ice Cream Parlor, a scoop of vanilla ice cream costs 50¢, a scoop of chocolate 55¢, and a scoop of strawberry 60¢. Yesterday afternoon, Kathy and five of her friends each bought a two-scoop ice-cream cone; no two of the six orders were identical. From the following information, determine each woman's full name (one surname is Sense), her order, and the price she paid, as well as the sequence in which the six orders were placed.

1. Jane is neither Ms. Drury nor Ms. Filler.

2. These four orders were taken consecutively, in this order: Ms. Kerr's, Marie's, Ms. Burke's, and Susan's.

3. Ms. Kerr's cone cost less than Ms. Burke's, which cost less than Ms. Filler's; Ms. Filler's order was not the fifth.

4. Ms. Rosten did not spend the most.

5. Four consecutive orders, in this order, were that of a woman who had at least one scoop of vanilla, Alice's, one that cost $1.10, and Ms. Drury's.

6. Rose, who wasn't the last to order, didn't pay the most.

7. Susan's cone cost less than the last one ordered, which cost less than the first one ordered.

The solution is on page 155.

1. _____
_____
_____
_____

2. _____
_____
_____
_____

3. _____
_____
_____
_____

4. _____
_____
_____
_____

5. _____
_____
_____
_____

6. _____
_____
_____
_____

57 CLASS REUNION

by Haydon Calhoun

Among the alumni attending Parnassus College's class reunion were Mary and six other close friends who now live in different cities around the country, including Houston. Each arrived on campus at a different hour from 1 p.m. to 7 p.m. on the Friday before Homecoming Weekend. From the clues that follow, determine each friend's full name (one surname is Kingston), hour of arrival, and home city.

1. While waiting for the other five to arrive, Ms. Quinlan (who isn't Golda) and Vera reminisced about "the good old, bad old days" of twenty years ago; among those they were awaiting were the Atlantan (who isn't Jim), the Philadelphian, and Walters.

2. Lon and Mr. Xavier arrived after 4 p.m., but neither of them arrived last.

3. When the Bostonian arrived, she told Mr. Zoltan and Rob, who isn't the Dallas man, how happy she was that they were there to greet her.

4. Ibbetson, who is from Chicago, arrived later than Ed, who is not from Atlanta or Dallas.

5. Ullman arrived later than the New Yorker, but not last.

6. Rob did not arrive at 5 p.m.

7. Walters' first name is neither Golda nor Jim.

The solution is on page 155.

	Ed	Golda	Jim	Lon	Mary	Rob	Vera	Atl.	Bos.	Chic.	Dal.	Hous.	NY	Phil.	1	2	3	4	5	6	7
Ibbet.																					
King.																					
Quin.																					
Ull.																					
Walt.																					
Xav.																					
Zolt.																					
1														
2														
3														
4														
5														
6														
7														
Atl.							
Bos.							
Chic.							
Dal.							
Hous.							
NY							
Phil.							

	Name	City
1		
2		
3		
4		
5		
6		
7		

58 MEAL PLANNING MADE EASY

by Mary A. Powell

During a coffee break one Friday afternoon, five women at Acme Products were discussing the difficulties of managing household chores. One detested laundry, another cleaning, but all agreed that cooking would be easier if only they didn't have to plan meals. "Why not trade ideas?" Marie suggested. "If each of us planned only one meal next week, we'd have enough to get us through the work week." They all agreed, and on Monday morning, each woman brought in her favorite recipe, and all five prepared it at some time during the week. From the following clues, can you find the full name of each woman (one last name is Pressley), the meal each planned (one was spaghetti), and the dinner each prepared each evening that week (Monday through Friday)?

1. No two prepared the same meal on any one night.

2. Ellen served her own planned meal on Tuesday, meat loaf on Wednesday, and Ms. Landower's meal on Thursday.

3. Susan prepared her own planned meal Wednesday, Ms. Shoemaker's meal Tuesday, and stroganoff on Thursday.

4. Karen prepared her own planned meal on Friday, chili on Tuesday, and Ms. Sawyer's meal Monday.

5. Ms. White, who is not Jane, prepared tuna the day before Ellen.

6. Karen and the woman who planned chili both prepared stroganoff two days before tuna casserole.

7. The woman who planned meat loaf prepared it on Monday.

The solution is on page 156.

PLANNER	MON	TUES	WED	THURS	FRI

HIGH SCHOOLS

by Randall L. Whipkey

When Dr. Ed U. Cator was honored on his retirement in the late 1950s, he pointed with pride to the fact that six high schools, among them Monroe High, were opened during his long tenure as Summerset school superintendent, all in different years. One of the schools is on Bay Street. From the clues below, can you determine the year in which each school was opened and the street on which it is located?

1. The last of the six schools opened in 1955.

2. The high school on Hill Street opened eight years before Lincoln High School and thirteen years before Jackson High.

3. Madison High School opened four years after the school on Glen Street.

4. Jefferson High School wasn't the fifth to open.

5. None of the six opened during World War II, here considered the years 1941–45.

6. The high school on Canyon Street isn't Lincoln.

7. The school on River Street opened six years before Jefferson High but seven years after Washington High.

8. The school on Valley Street was opened during the pre-World War II era.

The solution is on page 156.

	year	high school	street
1	_____	_____	_____
2	_____	_____	_____
3	_____	_____	_____
4	_____	_____	_____
5	_____	_____	_____
6	_____	_____	_____

60 BICYCLE SAFETY

by Evelyn B. Rosenthal

Mr. Drew and five other men each has a child who owns a bicycle. When the fathers all met to make suggestions for greater safety recently, each suggested either a white sweater or a fluorescent belt, as well as either a reflector or white-painted wheels or both; no two men had the same combination of suggestions. From the following clues, can you find the suggestions made by each man, his child's name (one is Lee), and the suggestions that each child accepted?

1. The girls' fathers each proposed more suggestions than the boys'.

2. Each child rejected precisely one of his or her father's suggestions; only Ed and the Green child adopted an idea of another child's father.

3. Pat and the Jones child each accepted only one suggestion; the other four children each agreed to two.

4. Only Fred agreed to wear a fluorescent belt, and only the March child agreed to both a reflector and white-painted wheels.

5. Only Hal and the Sims child accepted exactly the same suggestions.

6. Neither Mr. Brown, who made three suggestions, nor Mr. Sims urged a fluroescent belt.

7. The March child's first name is neither Ann nor Ed.

8. One and only one child thought that a reflector alone would suffice.

The solution is on page 157.

Use this space for solving.

PUZZLE FUN WITH DELL

by Margaret Shoop

Mr. and Mrs. Brown and their three children all love to solve puzzles, and each has a different favorite. Recently, a new copy of a Dell magazine provided fun for all of them. First one, then another, used the magazine to solve one of his or her favorite puzzles. From the information that follows, can you deduce the order in which the five used the magazine, the kind of puzzle each member of the family solved (one solved a page of Word Arithmetic puzzles), and how long it took?

1. Mrs. Brown used the magazine to solve a puzzle before Barbara did. Each of the two required the same amount of time to solve her puzzle, a time requirement different from that of any other family member.

2. Gary, who was the last to use the magazine, isn't the one who did the Solicross; he took twice as long to solve his puzzle as the family member who did an expert-level crossword.

3. The Anacrostic was done in an hour; it was solved just before a puzzle that took two hours and just after Mr. Brown had solved a puzzle.

4. The first person to use the magazine, who wasn't Mr. Brown, solved a Logic Problem.

5. Together, the five family members took 9½ hours to solve the five puzzles; each spent at least an hour on his or her puzzle.

6. Mrs. Brown didn't solve the crossword.

7. Mr. Brown needed more time than Alan.

The solution is on page 158.

	solver	puzzle	time
1			
2			
3			
4			
5			

62 BUTTON WILLOW'S GARDENERS

by Mary A. Powell

Most of the gardeners in Button Willow are quite casual about planting things, so their spring and summer flower gardens provide interesting and sometimes surprising color combinations. A few, however, are very precise about color arrangements and diligently mark everything. When it was time to dig up and put away the spring and summer flowering bulbs (and corns and rhizomes, which from now on will be called bulbs), five of these precise gardeners separated their bulbs by color as well as type and put them into carefully labeled boxes. Only one type and one color was kept in a single box. Since bulbs are prolific in Button Willow, each of these five gardeners had bulbs to share with the other four (one had yellow crocus bulbs). From the following clues, can you find what bulbs each gardener gave away (color and type), and what bulbs each gardener received?

1. Each gardener gave away two boxes of bulbs and received two boxes of bulbs.

2. George received one box of bulbs from Jonathan and another box from Megan.

3. Sabrina received a purple-flowering bulb from Jonathan and a white-flowering bulb from Ann.

4. The woman who gave away yellow tulip bulbs received yellow daffodil bulbs.

5. The gardener who gave away red amaryllis bulbs received no purple-flowering bulbs.

6. The gardener who gave away white narcissus bulbs received white iris bulbs.

7. The man who gave away purple crocus bulbs received purple hyacinth bulbs.

8. The gardener who gave away purple iris bulbs received red tulip bulbs.

9. Each gardener gave away two different colors; the two Megan gave away were the same two colors she received; the two colors George gave away were both different from the two he received.

The solution is on page 158.

Gardener	Gave		Received	

63   ALL-STARS

by Randall L. Whipkey

Among the players on the Eastern Division team in this year's Cozy Baseball League all-star game were Adams, Barnes, Carver, Dailey, and Edmonds. Each has made the all-star team a different number of times; their years as players in the League all differ as well. From the following clues, can you determine each player's position, his first and last name, how many years (in whole numbers) he has been in the league, and how many times he has made the all-star team?

1. The five players have been in the league a collective total of thirty years, and have been named to the all-stars a total of twenty-three seasons.

2. Mickey has been in the league two years longer than Adams, who has been in the league twice as long as the player who has been on the all-star team three times.

3. Harry has been in the league two years longer than the shortstop, who has been in the league twice as long as the two-time all-star.

4. Kerry has been an all-star two more times than Dailey, who is not the shortstop; neither is the left fielder.

5. Len's last name is not Barnes.

6. John plays neither shortstop nor left field.

7. Harry, whose surname is not Adams or Dailey, has made the all-stars four times.

8. The pitcher has been in the league longer than the catcher, who has been in the league longer than the first baseman.

9. The three-time all-star has been in the league longer than Edmonds.

The solution is on page 159.

years in league			all-star		
_____	_____	___	_____	_____	___
_____	_____	___	_____	_____	___
_____	_____	___	_____	_____	___
_____	_____	___	_____	_____	___
_____	_____	___	_____	_____	___

64 MEMORY RETENTION EXPERIMENT

by Margaret Shoop

In a controlled experiment in memory retention disguised as a card trick, a group of five psychology students was shown these six spades from an ordinary deck of 52 cards: the three, the four, the seven, the nine, the jack and the queen. The cards were first shuffled, then were shown one by one to the group. Each card was shown for a period of five seconds, then was placed face down so that it was no longer visible. Later the subjects were shown the cards in their natural order and were asked to write down the order in which they had seen them shown by the experimenter. The reports of the students were as follows:

	1st	2nd	3rd	4th	5th	6th
Bob	7	Q	J	4	9	3
Dave	7	J	Q	9	4	3
Eve	4	7	9	Q	J	3
Gloria	7	4	9	Q	J	3
Hal	7	4	9	Q	3	J

After he had examined their answers, the experimenter told the students: (1) No two of them had made the same number of correct placements; (2) each card had been correctly placed by at least one student; and (3) Gloria had made more correct placements than Hal. From these facts can you deduce the order in which the six cards had been shown?

The solution is on page 160.

65 FROM A TO Z

by Robert E. Nelson

Adam Zaklan and his wife Eve wanted as many children as possible. They gave their first child a name that began with "A" and went as far through the alphabet as possible, naming each successive child with the next letter of the alphabet. Although they didn't reach their ultimate goal of "Z," their children decided to carry on the tradition, so each grandchild (of Adam and Eve) was given a name starting with the next unused letter of the alphabet. At Adam and Eve's 40th anniversary party, children and grandchildren (there were no great-grandchildren yet) with names beginning with every letter of the alphabet (but no more) were present. From the following clues, determine which of Adam and Eve's children parented which of their grandchildren. Each of their children had at least one child.

1. "B" had more children than "C," who had more than "D."

2. The child with the fewest children did not have any of the last six.

3. There were at least two births to other children between each of the births of the child with the most children. The child with the second-most children had his or her first three in alphabetic sequence; however, at least two other children had at least two children each before this child had his/her fourth child.

4. The most children any parent had (including Adam and Eve) was seven, and each parent (including Adam and Eve) had a different number of children.

5. The first child didn't have the first grandchild, the second child the second grandchild, etc.

6. No child with a name beginning with a vowel had a child whose name began with a vowel (including Y). Only one child whose name began with a consonant had any children whose names began with consonants.

7. The youngest child of Adam and Eve had a number of children equal to the difference between the number of children "A" and "C" had.

The solution is on page 160.

CHILDREN

A	A	A	A	A	A	A
B	B	B	B	B	B	B
C	C	C	C	C	C	C
D	D	D	D	D	D	D
E	E	E	E	E	E	E
F	F	F	F	F	F	F
G	G	G	G	G	G	G
H	H	H	H	H	H	H
I	I	I	I	I	I	I
J	J	J	J	J	J	J
K	K	K	K	K	K	K
L	L	L	L	L	L	L
M	M	M	M	M	M	M
N	N	N	N	N	N	N
O	O	O	O	O	O	O
P	P	P	P	P	P	P
Q	Q	Q	Q	Q	Q	Q
R	R	R	R	R	R	R
S	S	S	S	S	S	S
T	T	T	T	T	T	T
U	U	U	U	U	U	U
V	V	V	V	V	V	V
W	W	W	W	W	W	W
X	X	X	X	X	X	X
Y	Y	Y	Y	Y	Y	Y
Z	Z	Z	Z	Z	Z	Z

GRANDCHILDREN

CHALLENGER LOGIC PROBLEMS

66 BUT WHERE'S HER HORSE?

by Robert E. Nelson

At Henri LaPhoux's first art gallery exhibition, the critics praised his painting "Lady Godiva at Rest" as an outstanding example of its genre. The painting was composed of a 5′ by 5′ grid of squares; four squares were blue, four were green, four were red, four were yellow, one was black, and the remaining eight were white. From the following clues, can you identify the color of each square in the painting?

1. No row or column had two squares of any color other than white; every row and column had at least one white square, but none had three or more.

2. Rows 2 and 4 and Columns A and D all had the same combination of colored squares.

3. No two squares of the same color other than white met at sides or corners.

4. Row 5 and Column E had the same combination of colored squares, but Row 1 does not have the same combination of colors as any column.

5. Every colored square other than white abutted at least one white square, but none abutted more than two.

6. Each of the diagonals had two blue squares in them.

7. Only two white squares abutted one another; they did not do so along the edge of the picture (i.e., only one, if either, was in Row 1 or 5 or Column A or E).

8. Row 3 had no red square and Column B had no green square.

The solution is on page 161.

The solution is on page 161.

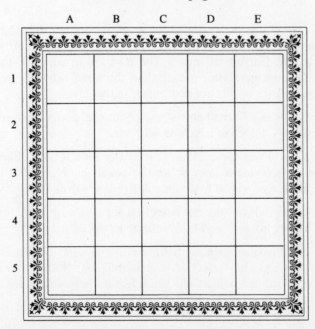

67 DETECTIVE DEDUCTION

by David Champlin

Mr. Hugh Dunnit belongs to a book club that sends each of its members a new novel of mystery and suspense each month. Mr. Dunnit noticed that, by an odd coincidence, the last names of each of the six authors of the books for January through June began with the same letter as one of the other authors' first names. Upon further investigation, Mr. Dunnit found that each of the six fictional detectives featured in the novels also had a last name that began with the same letter as one of the other detectives' first names. Each of the six novels (one of which is "Dinner á la Deadly") is set in a different foreign metropolis (one is set in Nairobi). From the clues given below, determine the full name of each author (one is Mr. Mitchell), the title and locale of the book he or she wrote, the full name of the detective featured in each novel (one first name is Katerina) and the month in which that book was the club selection.

1. The mystery Rosemary wrote, which was neither the January nor April selection, was sent to Mr. Dunnit earlier than the novel set in Budapest.

2. The novel in which the detective is named Angela was the selection for the month after the novel set in Moscow, and two months earlier than the novel set in Istanbul.

3. The six novels were, in no particular order: the selection for April; the novel set in Singapore; "Internationally Intriguing"; the novel in which the detective's first name is Thomas; the novel Gregory wrote, and the novel by Mr. Rockford.

4. Vanessa (who is not Ms. Trefoyle) is the detective who appeared in the May selection.

5. Elizabeth's novel was the selection for an earlier month than the novel set in Rio de Janeiro. "Murder Most Macabre" was the selection two months earlier than Mr. Carruthers' novel. The mystery in which Thomas appears was the selection for a later month than the novel whose detective is Ms. Armstrong. (All six novels are mentioned in this clue.)

6. Michael (who is not Carruthers) wrote about the sleuth whose last name is Banks. Inwood's detective is surnamed King.

7. Ellsworth's novel was the selection for a later month than "Silent Stalker," but for an earlier month than either the novel set in Istanbul or the novel where the detective whose first name is Bradley solves the mystery.

8. Carmen's novel (which was the selection for a later month than "Foreign Fatalities") does not feature Ms. Valentine as the detective.

9. Garland's novel (which does not feature either Bradley or Ms. Trefoyle as its detective) was the club selection one month earlier than the novel about Simon's crime solving, which was the selection before (but not immediately

114

before) the novel Ivan wrote (which is neither "Thrilled to Death" nor the June selection).

10. Standish, who is not Thomas, does not solve the mystery set in Budapest.

The solution is on page 162.

Month	Author			Detective		City	Title
	first	last		first	last		
___	___	___		___	___	___	___
___	___	___		___	___	___	___
___	___	___		___	___	___	___
___	___	___		___	___	___	___
___	___	___		___	___	___	___
___	___	___		___	___	___	___

68 WHO'S ON FIRST— AND IN ROOM 201?

by Randall L. Whipkey

When the Summerset County girls all-star softball team played in the national tournament last summer, the players stayed at the Guild Inn, with the ten starters in the adjacent double rooms 201, 203, 205, 207, and 209. Each all-star is from a different county school (one from Glenecho High), and played a different position: four were infielders (1B, 2B, SS, 3B), three outfielders (LF, CF, RF), and the others were pitcher (P), catcher (C), and designated hitter (DH). Given the clues below, can you make the nightly 11:00 bed check by finding the full names (one first name is Ingrid and one surname Kelly), positions, and high schools of the all-star pair in each room?

1. Two infielders shared a room, but the SS wasn't one of them.

2. The Randallstown High star didn't play 3B or LF.

3. The SS and her roommate were in 209; they weren't next door to Miss Nolan and her roommate.

4. Neither Abby nor Farrah was the all-star 3B.

5. Miss James and the Central High athlete were in different rooms.

6. Miss Mills and her roommate were in 207; they weren't next door to the Randallstown High star and her roommate.

7. The P and RF shared a room.

8. The LF and her roommate had room 201.

9. Farrah and her roommate had the room between those of Miss Nolan and her roommate and the Randallstown High star and her roommate.

10. Miss Mills, who isn't the Shakespeare High athlete, didn't play RF on the team.

11. When the coach did a room check, she started at one end of the hall with the room shared by Jackie and her roommate, then skipped two rooms before going to the room shared by Abby Lewis and her roommate, then went next door to the room where the 1B was a roommate.

12. Bobbi and her roommate had the room between those of the Shakespeare High star and her roommate and the 3B and hers.

13. Miss Riley shared a room with the DH.

14. Neither Farrah nor Bobbi was the all-star 2B.

15. Miss Nolan, who isn't Bobbi, and the 3B weren't roommates.

16. Farrah and the Shakespeare High star were in different rooms.

17. These three pairs of players shared adjacent rooms in consecutive ascending order: Darla and her roommate, Heather and hers, and the Berlin High athlete and hers.

116

18. Christy's room was next door to that of Miss James, who isn't Gina.

19. Gina and the C from Wildlake High shared a room—not 209.

20. Jackie played neither LF nor DH.

21. Jackie and Miss Quinn jogged every morning to loosen up.

22. The athlete from Berlin High wasn't the all-star SS.

23. Miss Owens, who isn't Christy and who wasn't the all-star CF, and the Fillmore High athlete play on the same club team during the summer.

24. Erin, who wasn't the team's DH, had the room next door to that of the Easthills High star and her roommate.

25. Miss Price and the Vo-Tech athlete shared a room.

26. Miss Scott, who didn't represent Fillmore High, and her roommate had the room between those of Miss Owens and her roommate and the Ocean City High star and hers.

The solution is on page 162.

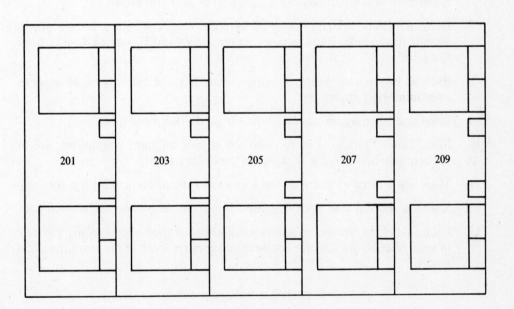

201   203   205   207   209

69 BROWN'S DAIRY

by Robert E. Nelson

Vic and Vera Brown are a young farm couple who have a herd of 20 dairy cows. From the milk, they make cheese that they sell every Saturday at a local farmers' market. Monica, Sandra, and their other 18 cows have colorations of either all black, all brown, black with white spots, or brown with white spots. The stanchions in the Browns' milking barn are arranged in a square with five cows on each side and are numbered in clockwise order. From the following clues, identify the name and coloration of the cow in each stanchion.

1. No one side of the square has two cows with alphabetically sequential names.

2. Alice, Elsie, Iris, and Odette, who are of four different colorations, are on different sides of the square.

3. Numerically, on one side of the square, the cows are in alphabetical order; on the opposite side, they are in reverse alphabetical order.

4. Betty, Jewel, Lola, and Rose, who are of four different colorations, are all on one side of the square.

5. No two cows of the same coloration are in numerically adjacent stanchions except for those in numbers 7 and 8; all the cows on that side have solid colors.

6. A different number of cows has each of the four colorations, but the same number are all or partially black as are all or partially brown.

7. Gertrude, Paula, and Toni, who all have the same coloration, are all on one side of the square. Paula is twice as far away from Hester as Toni is from Queenie.

8. Each all-brown cow is directly opposite another; the majority of those are in even-numbered stanchions.

9. Jewel and Iris have the same coloration; so do Betty and Cora.

10. Cora, Dora, Flora, and Nora, who are of four different colorations, are in sequentially numbered stanchions in the order named.

11. There are at least as many all-black cows as spotted cows of both colors.

12. Karen, a spotted cow, is in stanchion 14 next to Alice, another spotted cow.

13. Each side of the square has a different number of spotted cows; only one pair of spotted cows are directly opposite one another (both of these are the same color).

The solution is on page 163.

118

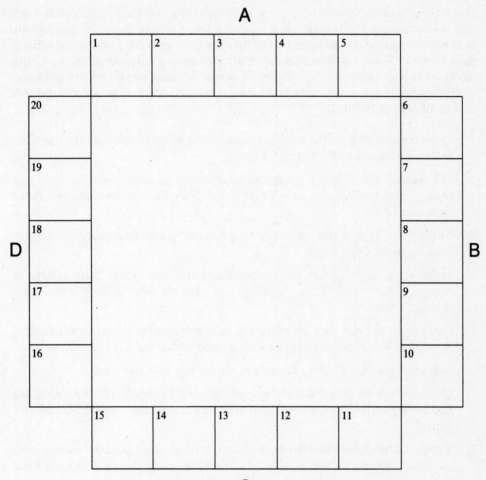

70 NIFTY NAPKINS

by Mary Marks Cezus

Five women recently studied the art of napkin folding and each demonstrated her new skill at a party she hosted. Each woman chose just one shape for the napkins at her party and no two women folded their napkins into the same shapes. Each party had a different number of guests and celebrated a different occasion. Using the clues below, can you determine each woman's name, napkin shape, occasion celebrated (one was a welcome home party), and number of guests (five, eight, twelve, fifteen, or twenty)?

1. The woman who gave the graduation party had more guests than the one who folded her napkins into bishops' caps.

2. The woman who folded her napkins to resemble pineapples (which were not used at the anniversary party) and Carly both like to read articles about entertaining.

3. Neither Wallis nor the woman who gave the graduation party folded her napkins to look like swans.

4. There were more guests at the birthday party than there were guests at Yvonne's party and the party where the napkins were folded to resemble rabbits combined.

5. Carly (who did not give the party which celebrated the publication of a first novel) had fewer guests than the woman who folded her napkins into swans.

6. Neither Wallis nor Mallory folded her napkins to look like ducks.

7. The woman who gave the party to celebrate the publication of the first novel had more guests than Jody (who did not fold her napkins to resemble bishops' caps).

8. Yvonne (who did not fold her napkins into bishops' caps) and the woman who gave the anniversary party (which did not have the napkins which resembled rabbits) both planned their parties for several weeks.

9. Neither Mallory nor the woman who folded her napkins to look like pineapples gave the party to celebrate the publication of a first novel.

The solution is on page 164.

Name	Shape	Occasion	# of Guests

71 GULLIBLE'S TRAVELS

by Randall L. Whipkey

In his classic novel "Gullible's Travels," Jonathan Fast describes the adventures of the ship-wrecked Samuel Gullible, who visits five different foreign lands before finally sailing back to his native England. Each land visited has a different eccentric leader and has citizens with an unusual characteristic—in one, the people are all matchstick thin. From this and the chronicle below, can you chart Gullible's itinerary: the name of each strange land's ruler, the peculiar characteristic of its natives, the order in which Gullible visits the five in his travels, and how he leaves each one?

1. Immediately after being ridden out of Altupa on the shoulders of an angry mob, Gullible enters the land where the natives are all pedagogical teachers.

2. After escaping from Tullipil in a hot-air balloon, Gullible immediately lands in the nation whose citizens are intelligent bovines.

3. Gullible is in the land of Bordingbang right after visiting the country headed by Prime Minister Jingleheimer.

4. The natives of Emperor Dramaticus's realm, which isn't Monshynhuh, aren't the foolish magicians.

5. Gullible enters the country of Oldaag by riding a log raft out of King Tat II's kingdom.

6. Tullipil isn't home to either the pedagogues or the 400-lb.'ers.

7. After being forced to flee the foolish magicians on the back of an elephant, Gullible rides into the land ruled by Chief Moomador.

8. The nation populated by citizens weighing 400 lbs. isn't ruled by King Tat II.

9. Bordingbang isn't home to the 400-lb.'ers.

10. Queen Leeahh's realm isn't the fourth one visited by Gullible in his travels.

The solution is on page 165.

#	country	ruler	characteristic	mode of departure
1				
2				
3				
4				
5				

72 THE SAFE-HOUSE PROJECT

by Claudia Strong

Last week, Bonnie and eleven other women who had volunteered to offer their homes as neighborhood safe houses met at Central Avenue School to finalize plans for the project. Each was given a glow-in-the-dark placard to place on her front door to identify it, and each was assigned a number #1 to #12 as shown in the diagram opposite. From the clues that follow, can you determine the full name of each of the twelve volunteers, where each woman lives in the neighborhood, and how each got to the meeting? (NOTE: In determining turns, *driveways* are not counted.)

1. Both Paula and one of the women who live on Teakwood Place walked their children to Ms. Fenwick's house, where the Fenwick teenagers babysat for the younger children; all three women then car pooled to the meeting in Ms. Fenwick's car without making any other stops.

2. Esther's safe house was assigned the number one lower than Bella's.

3. Flo (who is neither Truitt nor Agner) had to drive farther north to pick up her friend Ms. McCrea than she would have had she gone straight from her house to the school.

4. Ms. Cushing and June both live on the same side of Central Avenue, but Ms. Cushing lives more to the south than June.

5. The Slayton house is next door to Louise's house.

6. Trudy lives directly across the street from Ms. Reid but, because she was running very late that day, Trudy drove alone to the meeting.

7. Frances and Ms. Agner each drove to the meeting, and each made three turns before reaching the school.

8. The safe house which Ms. Kozak (whose first name is not Flo) volunteered for was the only one to be set up on her street.

9. Three of the women bicycled together to the meeting. One of them was a Linden Way resident, the other two—Leah and Ms. Breck—live on two other streets on that same side of Central Avenue.

10. To get to the school, Beth always drives right by Ms. Garen's house (which is on another street), so Beth gave her a ride to the meeting that day.

11. Ms. Wiggins' safe house number was one higher than Ms. Horne's.

12. Ms. Agner and Trudy both live on the same side of Central Avenue.

13. Ellen lives on the north side of the same street as Ms. Truitt (who is not June).

14. No one had to cross Central Avenue to become involved in a car pool.

The solution is on page 166.

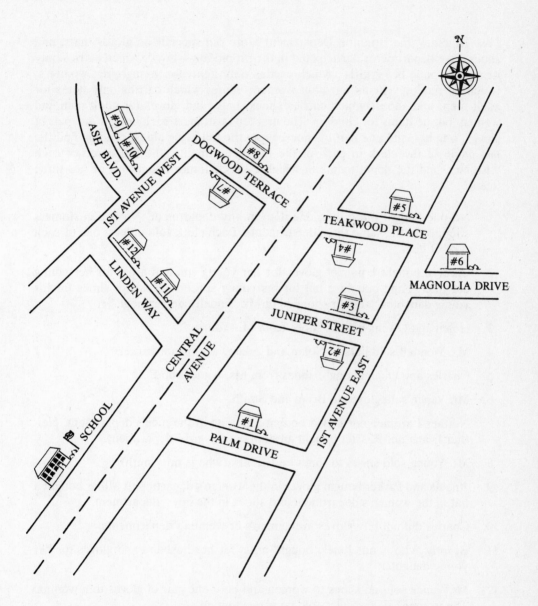

73 GLOVES, HATS, AND SHOES

by Mary A. Powell

Last Thursday, the Brighton Department Store ran specials on gloves, hats, and shoes. Five departments participated in the promotion—boys', which carries only items for young boys; girls', which carries only items for young girls; women's, which carries only items for adult women; men's, which carries only items for adult men; and shoes, which carries shoes, hats, and gloves for adult men and women, but no items for children. The first ten customers each bought one pair of gloves, one hat, and one pair of shoes. From the following clues, can you find the last name of the clerk in each of the five departments, the full name of each customer, and the departments in which each customer bought his or her three items?

1. No one bought more than one item in any department. No two customers shopped in the same three departments. Each clerk sold at least one of each type of item.

2. Carolyn bought a pair of gloves for her young son and a hat for her young daughter. King bought a hat for his young son and a pair of shoes for his young daughter. Neither shopped in Ms. Tindall's department.

3. Helen and Owens bought shoes from Mr. Young.

4. Ms. Wendell sold hats to Nolan and Adam, who is not Parker.

5. Charles and Queen bought shoes from Ms. Underwood.

6. Mr. Vance sold gloves to Brian and Smith.

7. Neither Lattimer nor David bought anything in the men's department. Neither Diane nor Ressler bought anything in the girls' department.

8. Mr. Young sold shoes to Jones and Henry (who is not Smith).

9. Angela and Parker bought gloves in the women's department; Miller bought a hat in the women's department and shoes in the boys' department.

10. Charles did not buy gloves in the men's or women's departments.

11. Beverly, who is not Jones, bought a hat for her husband and gloves for her young daughter.

12. Mr. Vance sold no shoes to women and only one pair of gloves to a woman. The women's department sold no shoes to men.

13. Ms. Underwood sold one more hat than the clerk in the shoe department and one less than the clerk in the boys' department.

14. The clerk in the shoe department sold three more pairs of shoes than Ms. Tindall. The clerk in the women's department sold two more pairs of gloves than Ms. Underwood.

15. The girls' department sold three times as many shoes as gloves. Ms. Wendell's department sold three times as many hats as pairs of shoes.

The solution is on page 167.

Salesperson					
department					
# of hats					
# of gloves					
# of shoes					

Customers:

_____

_____

_____

_____

_____

_____

_____

_____

_____

74 DOG DAYS

by Robert E. Nelson

When Kenton Kennels opened as a dog boarding business, it had ten caged runs located side by side and numbered 1–10. It opened on a Monday, but no dogs were brought in that day. By Saturday evening, however, it had a dog in each run; one or more dogs had been brought in each day Tuesday through Saturday and all of them were still there. From the following clues, identify the dog in each cage, its breed (one was a Great Dane), the full name of its owner (one was Mr. Lang); and the day on which it was brought to the kennel.

1. The beagle and Carol's dog were at opposite ends of the row of runs.

2. In sequentially higher numbered runs, six of the dogs were: the Dalmatian, a dog brought in Saturday, Ranger, Mr. Owens' (who was not Ivan) dog, a dog brought in Wednesday, and Edna's dog.

3. More dogs were brought in Thursday than any other day and fewer were brought in Saturday than any other day. Neither Blaze nor the spitz nor George's dog, nor Miss Upham's dog was brought in either of those days, but one or more of them was brought in each of the other days.

4. Lucky and the pointer were owned by men, while the Weimaraner and Tiny were owned by women. In the order named, these four dogs were in increasingly higher numbered, but not necessarily sequential, runs.

5. Alice's dog was between Mr. Rodman's and King.

6. The Irish setter, which was not Zippy, was brought in the day before Spot and the day after Miss McGee's dog. At least two runs separated each of these dogs.

7. No dogs brought in the same day were in adjacent runs.

8. The dogs named Duke, King, and Princess, none of which was the Irish setter, were (in some order) in adjacent runs, as were three other dogs owned by Betty (who was not Miss Quail), Frank, and Ivan. The run number of Betty's dog was twice that of Duke's.

9. In sequentially higher numbered runs, six of the dogs were: Henry's, Miss Nolan's, the German shepherd, a dog brought in Tuesday, Donna's, and Mr. Strang's.

10. Miss Perkins owned the collie and Miss Quail's dog was Missy.

11. The Newfoundland was owned by a man other than Mr. Owens.

12. John Trent brought his dog in on Thursday.

The solution is on page 169.

1

_____ _____ (owner)
_____ (dog, breed)
_____ (day)

2

_____ _____ (owner)
_____ (dog, breed)
_____ (day)

3

_____ _____ (owner)
_____ (dog, breed)
_____ (day)

4

_____ _____ (owner)
_____ (dog, breed)
_____ (day)

5

_____ _____ (owner)
_____ (dog, breed)
_____ (day)

6

_____ _____ (owner)
_____ (dog, breed)
_____ (day)

7

_____ _____ (owner)
_____ (dog, breed)
_____ (day)

8

_____ _____ (owner)
_____ (dog, breed)
_____ (day)

9

_____ _____ (owner)
_____ (dog, breed)
_____ (day)

10

_____ _____ (owner)
_____ (dog, breed)
_____ (day)

75 GOLF SCRAMBLE

by Mary A. Powell

Each month, Fairview Country Club's professional golf instructor takes eight of his students out for a 9-hole golf scramble. In this variation, the eight form two teams. Each member of a team tees off (hits the first shot) from the starting position, then the best shot of the four is chosen and each member shoots from that position. All four then hit from the location of each succeeding *best* shot until one team member putts the ball into the hole. The two teams play each hole this way, and the team with the FEWEST strokes wins the hole, with the winning team teeing off first on the next hole. In case of a tie, the team that won the previous hole continues as the first to tee off. The team with the LOWEST total score for all nine holes wins the game. From the following clues, can you find the full names of Mr. Parker and the other members of both teams in last week's golf scramble; identify the players who had the best tee shots and final putts on each of the nine holes; and determine each team's score on each hole, and the final score? (Note: Husbands and wives share the same surname.)

1. Two of the three married couples were Larry and his wife, who were on the same team, and the Listers, who were on different teams. Each team had two men.

2. Judy had two best tee shots and four final putts; two of her putts won the hole for her team.

3. All three of Mr. Smith's best tee shots came on holes before that on which he made his one final putt, which was not on the 9th hole.

4. Karen had two consecutive final putts.

5. On one team, each member had at least one best shot on each hole. On the other team, none of Arnold's shots were played on the 4th hole and none of Mrs. Parker's were played on the 8th hole; each team member had at least one best shot on all other holes.

6. The team with 45 total strokes won four holes. The 3rd and 5th holes were tied with five strokes each.

7. Ms. Field's team teed off first on the 4th and 7th holes. Dawn's team teed off first on the 2nd and 5th holes. Dawn is not Ms. Field.

8. On the 2nd, 4th, and 8th holes, both best tee shots were made by men; on all other holes, one man and one woman made the best tee shots. On the 1st, 2nd, 5th, and 8th holes, both final putts were made by women; on one hole, two men made the final putts; on four holes, one man and one woman made the final putts.

9. One of Mr. Monroe's best tee shots came three holes before his wife's only best tee shot, which was not on the 9th hole. One of Bob's best tee shots came three holes before his wife's only best tee shot.

10. Sandra, who had three best shots on the 8th hole, is not married to Larry.

11. Only one of Chester's two final putts was a winner.

130

12. Ms. Field, Sandra, Mrs. Lister, and Karen were four of the five who had the best tee shot *and* the final putt on one or more holes.

13. The highest score for either team on any one hole was seven; the lowest was three. Both scores were made on the same hole.

14. Larry and Mrs. Lister both had two best shots on the 7th hole; neither had the best tee shot or the final putt.

15. Neither Bob, Mr. Monroe, nor Sandra had the final putt on the 4th hole.

16. Karen didn't have the best tee shot or the final putt on the 1st hole.

17. Sandra was not the person who putted in the fifth shot for her team on the 7th hole.

18. Bob, who had the same number of best tee shots as Chester, did not have the best tee shots on the 6th or 7th holes.

19. Karen had twice as many final putts as Bob; Dawn had twice as many final putts as Larry.

20. On the 4th hole, the winners won by two strokes.

21. The winning team won the game by three strokes. The losing team won the 9th hole.

The solution is on page 170.

Hole	Team 1	Score	Team 2	Score
1	Tee: Putt:		Tee: Putt:	
2	Tee: Putt:		Tee: Putt:	
3	Tee: Putt:		Tee: Putt:	
4	Tee: Putt:		Tee: Putt:	
5	Tee: Putt:		Tee: Putt:	
6	Tee: Putt:		Tee: Putt:	
7	Tee: Putt:		Tee: Putt:	
8	Tee: Putt:		Tee: Putt:	
9	Tee: Putt:		Tee: Putt:	
TOTAL				

SOLVING HINT: Solve in this order—full names, teams, number of tees and putts each individual had, scores for each hole, final score, and finally, names of those who had tee shots and final putts on each hole.

131

SOLUTIONS

1. PUMPKIN CARVERS

Timothy did not make the moon (clue 1), the lion (clue 3), or the owl (clue 6), so he made the pirate. Timothy's pirate pumpkin was not purchased at Harvest of Plenty (clue 3), Friendly Acres (clue 2), or the Pie Patch (clue 4); he bought it at Autumn Bounty. The pumpkin purchased at Harvest of Plenty was not made into the moon (clue 1) or the lion (clue 3), so it was the owl. By clue 5, Patsy didn't make the owl or lion, so she made the moon. Roy didn't make the owl (clue 6), so Sally did and, by elimination, Roy made the lion. Roy did not buy his pumpkin at Friendly Acres (clue 2), so, by elimination, he bought his at the Pie Patch, and Patsy bought hers at Friendly Acres. In sum:

>Patsy, moon, Friendly Acres
>Roy, lion, Pie Patch
>Sally, owl, Harvest of Plenty
>Timothy, pirate, Autumn Bounty

2. HALLOWEEN PAGEANT

The star of Scene 1 was not the cat (clue 1), the skeleton (clue 3), or the ghost (clue 5); it was the pumpkin. By clue 5, then, the ghost appeared in Scene 2. Kim was not in the last scene (clue 2), nor were Lee or Trent (clue 3); that star performer was Sal. Since Sal didn't play the cat (clue 4), he played the skeleton, and the cat starred in Scene 3. Lee did not star as the pumpkin in Scene 1 (clue 3), nor did Kim (clue 2), so Trent did. By clue 3, then, Lee was in Scene 2, and, by elimination, Kim was in Scene 3. In sum:

>Scene 1: Trent, pumpkin
>Scene 2: Lee, ghost
>Scene 3: Kim, black cat
>Scene 4: Sal, skeleton

3. VITAL STATISTICS

The 35-year-old is not Alan (clue 1), Dave (clue 2), or Chuck (clue 4); he is Bill. Dave is 30 (clue 2). By clue 1, then, Chuck is 25 and Alan is 20. Bill is not 6'2" (clue 2) so, by clue 3, he is 6'0" and Chuck is 5'8". Alan is not 5'10" (clue 1), so Dave is; by elimination, Alan is 6'2". He weighs 225 pounds (clue 2). Chuck weighs 250 (clue 4). By clue 5, Dave does not weigh 175, so Bill does; by elimination, Dave weighs 200. In sum:

>Alan, 20, 6'2", 225
>Bill, 35, 6'0", 175
>Chuck, 25, 5'8", 250
>Dave, 30, 5'10", 200

4. SNOWY DAY ACTIVITIES

One boy is building the fort (clue 1) and the other boy is shoveling (clue 3), so the girls are sledding and making the snowman. The oldest child isn't building the fort (clue 1), making the snowman (clue 2), or shoveling snow (clue 3), so the oldest is the girl who is sledding. By clue 1, Zoe isn't the oldest, so Lana is, and Zoe is making the snowman. By clue 2, then, Rhett is ten, Zoe is eight, and the child in the blue jacket is six, who, by elimination, is Dirk. By clue 4, Rhett wears the yellow jacket. Also by clue 4, Rhett isn't shoveling, so Dirk is, and Rhett is building the fort. Lana doesn't have the red jacket (clue 3), so Zoe does, and, by elimination, Lana has the green jacket. In sum:

>Dirk, 6, shoveling, blue jacket
>Zoe, 8, making the snowman, red jacket
>Rhett, 10, building the fort, yellow jacket
>Lana, 12, sledding, green jacket

5. PHONETIC NAMES

"Jonquil" is the word formed phonetically by John Quill. By clue 1, Cliff and Hangor sound like "cliff-hanger," Joe and King form "joking," Claude and Hopper form "clodhopper," Barb and Dwyer form "barbed wire" and Otto and Matick form "automatic." By clue 2, Cliff planned to take German. John Quill is from Grass Valley (intro). By clue 3, Barb is from Tall Palms and Matick from Hilldale. Cliff's hometown isn't Templeton or Crestview (clue 2), so he is from Poker Flat. Joe was the last one to register (clue 4) so he isn't from Crestview (clue 2); he is from Templeton and Claude is from Crestview. By clue 5, King planned to take Russian and Hopper planned on Spanish. Neither Barb nor Otto wanted to take French (clue 3) so, by elimination, John is taking French. By clue 6, Otto wasn't interested in Italian so, by elimination, Barb was taking Italian and Otto was taking Portuguese. In sum:

Barb Dwyer	(barbed wire)	Tall Palms	Italian
Cliff Hangor	(cliffhanger)	Poker Flat	German
Claude Hopper	(clodhopper)	Crestview	Spanish
Joe King	(joking)	Templeton	Russian
Otto Matick	(automatic)	Hilldale	Portuguese
John Quill	(jonquil)	Grass Valley	French

6. BALLOON ANIMALS

The horse was red (clue 2). The dog was not blue or yellow (clue 5); it was green. The giraffe was not blue (clue 1), so it was yellow, and the cat was blue. Jane is not the King girl (clue 6), so Sara is King. Billy is not Bradley or Smith (clue 4), so Billy is Johnson. The child who received the blue cat was not Ken (clue 1), Sara (clue 2), or Billy Johnson (clue 3); Jane did. She is not Bradley (clue 2), so Ken is Bradley and Jane is Smith. Neither Ken Bradley nor Sara received the red horse (clue 2), so Billy did. Ken's animal wasn't the giraffe (clue 1), so he received the green dog, and Sara received the yellow giraffe. In summary:

> Ken Bradley, green dog
> Billy Johnson, red horse
> Sara King, yellow giraffe
> Jane Smith, blue cat

7. FESTIVAL BOOTHS

The first booth doesn't have the keychains (clue 1), the silk plants (clue 4), or the woodcrafts (clue 6); it features needlework. "Just Becuz" is either the first or second booth (clue 1), but it is not the first (clue 5); it is the second. By clue 1, the keychains are in the third booth and the yellow awning is on the fourth. The woodcrafts are not in the second booth (clue 6); they are in the fourth, and the silk plants are in the second. The green awning, then, is on the first booth (clue 4). The blue awning is not second (clue 2); it is third, and the red awning is second. "Magic Door" is in the fourth booth (clue 3). "Brilliance" is not in the third booth (clue 2); it is in the first, and "Stardrops" is in the third. In summary:

Brilliance Needlework Green	Just Becuz Silk plants Red	Stardrops Keychains Blue	Magic Door Woodcrafts Yellow

8. EAST-COAST VACATIONS

The woman going to Miami Beach is not Anna (clue 1), Denise (clue 2), or Betty (clue 3); she is Carol. The woman going to Washington, D.C., is neither Anna (clue 1) nor Denise (clue 2); she is Betty. Fred, then, is married to Carol (clue 3). The man going to Boston is neither Ed (clue 1) nor Hank (clue 2); he is Gary. By clue 1, the Lombards are going to either Washington, D.C., or Miami Beach; by clue 3, they are going to D.C. By clue 1, then, Anna is going to Boston and Ed is going to New York. By elimination, Denise is going to New York, while Hank is going to Washington. Neither the Ingersolls nor the Klines are going to Boston (clue 4), so the Johnstons are. Ed is not Mr. Kline (clue 4), so Fred is; by elimination, Ed is Mr. Ingersoll. In sum:

> Boston: Anna & Gary Johnston
> New York City: Denise & Ed Ingersoll
> Washington, D.C.: Betty & Hank Lombard
> Miami Beach: Carol & Fred Kline

9. TAKING CARE

Margaret has a son (clue 1). He is not Anthony (clue 5); he is Brett. The child who attends Small Wonder is not Brett or Crystal (clue 1), or Denise (clue 4); he is Anthony. Anthony's mother is neither Norma (clue 2) nor Lois (clue 4); she is Kate. The woman who takes her child to Tots Haven is neither Lois nor Margaret (clue 3); she is Norma. Margaret's son does not go to Kinder Kindness (clue 5); by elimination, he attends Lovin' Care, while Lois's child goes to Kinder Kindness. Margaret is not Simpson (clue 1), Rich (clue 2), or Talman (clue 3); she is Upshaw. Norma is neither Rich (clue 2) nor Talman (clue 3); she is Simpson. Denise is not Norma's daughter (clue 4); she is Lois's daughter, and Crystal is Norma's daughter. Lois is not Talman (clue 5); she is Rich, and Kate is Talman. In summary:

> Kate, Anthony, Talman, Small Wonder
> Lois, Denise, Rich, Kinder Kindness
> Margaret, Brett, Upshaw, Lovin' Care
> Norma, Crystal, Simpson, Tots Haven

10. SWEETS TO THE SWEET

Rolfe made the marzipan toys (clue 2). He did not make the chocolate swans (clue 4), roses (clue 6), chalet (clue 7), or butterflies (clue 9); he made the chocolate bunnies, and comes from Splugen (clue 4). His last name is not Scherer (clue 1); Hassler (clue 3), Tobler (clue 7), or Iselin (clue 8); he is Herr Luzi. Kurt's last name is Scherer, and he is not from Andeer (clue 1), Donath (clue 3), or Scharans (clue 5); he is from Zillis, and made the marzipan elves (clue 8) and chocolate butterflies (clue 9). Urs, who is from Scharans (clue 5), made the marzipan fruit (clue 9). He did not make the roses (clue 6) or swans (clue 4); he made the chocolate chalet, and his last name is Tobler (clue 7). Otto made the chocolate swans (clue 4) and, by elimination, Bert made the roses and marzipan animals (clue 6). By elimination, Otto made the marzipan clowns, so his last name is Iselin (clue 8). He is not from Donath (clue 3), so he is from Andeer. By elimination, Bert is Herr Hassler from Donath. In summary:

> Bert Hassler, Donath: chocolate roses & marzipan animals
> Kurt Scherer, Zillis: chocolate butterflies and marzipan elves
> Otto Iselin, Andeer: chocolate swans and marzipan clowns
> Rolfe Luzi, Splugen: chocolate bunnies & marzipan toys
> Urs Tobler, Scharans: chocolate chalet & marzipan fruit

11. FORTUNE SEEKERS

All six of the fortune seekers are mentioned in clue 1; the three who came by wagon train were Peron, the Dutchman, and the one who started a barber shop. By clue 2, Meer and Joe Ricardo came by wagon train, so Meer, who established a grocery store, must be the Dutchman, and Joe Ricardo started the barber shop. As Peron, Meer, and Ricardo traveled by wagon train, Burns, Wilson, and Maloney arrived by ship and (by clue 1) are Bob, the livery stable owner, and the Irishman. By clue 5, Cal Wilson, the Welshman, established the livery stable. By clue 6, Tim and Burns traveled by ship, so Tim is the Irishman and Burns is Bob while, by elimination, Tim is Maloney. By clue 3, Paul started a laundry; he is Peron, and, by elimination, Hal is Meer. By clue 4, the Scotsman started a foundry, so he is Burns and, by elimination, Maloney started a restaurant. By clue 7, Joe is not French, so he is Italian and Paul is French. In sum:

> Bob Burns, Scottish, foundry
> Tim Maloney, Irish, restaurant
> Hal Meer, Dutch, grocery
> Paul Peron, French, laundry
> Joe Ricardo, Italian, barber
> Cal Wilson, Welsh, livery

12. FINE ARTISTS

First honorable mention was won by the artist from Eastburg (clue 5). Second honorable mention did not go to the artist from Southlawn (clue 1), Weston (clue 3), or Northville (clue 4); so its winner is from Midland. By clues 1 and 4, the first-prize winner is not from Southlawn or Northville. This winner was not Adele (clue 1), Arty (clue 4), Ann (clue 6), or Alice (clue 8); Andy was the first-prize winner, and comes from Weston. He does not specialize in sculpture (clue 1), charcoal (clue 3), still life (clue 4), or portraits (clue 6); he does seascapes. By clue 1, then, four artists placed ahead of the sculptor, so the sculptor is the second-honorable-mention artist from Midland, and the charcoal artist took second prize. By clue 4, then, the still life took first honorable mention, Arty took third prize, and the charcoal artist is from Northville. By elimination, Arty is from Southlawn and paints portraits. Adele is neither the charcoal artist nor the sculptor (clue 1); she is the still-life artist. Alice is not from Northville (clue 8), so she is the Midland sculptor while Ann, by elimination, is the charcoal artist. By clues 2 and 6, Andy's, Ann's, and Arty's last name are neither Black nor Brown; Adele is not Black (clue 5), so she is Brown, and Alice is Black. By clue 7, Arty is White. Andy is not Gray (clue 8); he is Gold, and Ann is Gray. In sum:

> First prize—Andy Gold, seascapes, Weston
> Second prize—Ann Gray, charcoal, Northville
> Third prize—Arty White, portraits, Southlawn
> First honorable mention—Adele Brown, still life, Eastburg
> Second honorable mention—Alice Black, sculpture, Midland

13. NEW PERFUME

By clues 1 and 2, the six employees are: the three who came in the carpool—the person who suggested *Evening Star,* Sally, and Downs; the two who came by bus—Juan and the person from Research; and the man from Administration who walks. Harry, who works in Marketing and suggested the name *Mystique* (clue 3), is Mr. Downs from the carpool. By clue 7, Evans rides a bus to work and works in Finance, so he is Juan. By clue 6, Nell uses the bus and so is in Research; she suggested the name *Foofu.* By clue 4, Carl Hart, who suggested the name *Pixie,* is the walker from the Administration Department. Tom, by elimination, is the one who suggested *Evening Star.* Booth, the woman who works in Personnel (clue 5), is Sally, and Tom, by elimination, works in Supply. *Moon Mist* was not suggested by Juan (clue 8), so that was Sally's suggestion, while Juan suggested *Amber.* Nell's name is not Carroll (clue 6), so she is Gamble, and Tom is Carroll. In sum:

> Sally Booth, Personnel, *Moon Mist*
> Tom Carroll, Supply *Evening Star*
> Harry Downs, Marketing, *Mystique*
> Juan Evans, Finance, *Amber*
> Nell Gamble, Research, *Foofu*
> Carl Hart, Administration, *Pixie*

14. HOUSE OF GARDENS

There are two boys (Basil and Herb) and three girls (Flora, Violet, and Daisy) in the family. The youngest child is a girl (clue 4) and the other two girls are older than Herb (clue 3). Basil, who does not live in the pink or yellow room (clue 7), the lavender room (clue 3) or the green room (clue 5) lives in the blue room. By clue 2, he is not the oldest child, so one of the girls is. This girl is neither Daisy nor Violet (clue 6), so she is Flora. Since Violet is younger than Daisy (clue 6), she is the youngest child. Herb is younger than both Daisy and Flora (clue 3), so he is the second-youngest. Daisy is younger than her other brother Basil (clue 6), so she is the third-oldest child, and Basil is second-oldest. By clue 6, Herb is the comic collector. Violet has the Alton Jon poster in her room (clue 4) so, by clue 2, Daisy is the child with the poster of Scarfield the Cat. By clue 3, Flora has the Whitney Dallas poster, while Daisy's room is painted lavender. Herb's room is then green (clue 7). Basil does not have the He-Boy poster in his room (clue 6), so Herb does and Basil has the Cricketman poster. Violet's room is not yellow (clue 4) so Flora's is, and Violet has the pink room. Neither Flora (clue 1), Violet (clue 4), nor Basil (clue 5) collects teddy bears; Daisy does. Neither Basil (clue 5) nor Flora (clue 1) collects butterflies, so Violet does. Flora is the girl who collects picture postcards (introduction) and Basil, by elimination, collects stamps. In sum:

> Flora's yellow room holds picture postcards and a poster of Whitney Dallas.
> Basil's blue room holds stamps and a poster of Cricketman.
> Daisy's lavender room holds teddy bears and a poster of Scarfield the Cat.
> Herb's green room holds comic books and a poster of He-Boy.
> Violet's pink room holds butterflies and a poster of Alton Jon.

15. MAY BASKETS

By clue 1, four of the five are: Susan, Ms. Little, the one who received carnations, and the one who lives in Montana, who is not Jane. Jane received tulips and is not Ms. Little (clue 2), so she is the fifth woman. Ms. Thompson, who lives in California and received violets (clue 3), is Susan. The one who lives in Ohio and did not receive carnations or tulips (clue 4) is Ms. Little. By clue 5, Jane is neither Ms. Olstad nor the one who lives in Wisconsin, so Jane lives in Alaska, Ms. Olstad lives in Montana, and the one who received carnations lives in Wisconsin. By clues 5 and 6, Trudy is neither Ms. Olstad nor the one who lives in Wisconsin, so she is Ms. Little from Ohio. Also by clue 6, Trudy didn't receive the daisies, so she received the roses and Ms. Olstad received the daisies. By the same clue, then, Ms. Olstad is not Sharon, so she is Barb, and Sharon is the one in Wisconsin. Sharon is not Ms. Lansing (clue 7), so she is Ms. Kohn, and Jane is Lansing. In sum:

> Sharon Kohn, Wisconsin, carnations
> Jane Lansing, Alaska, tulips
> Trudy Little, Ohio, roses
> Barb Olstad, Montana, daisies
> Susan Thompson, California, violets

16. PAR FOR THE COURSE

The four women are: the golfer who shot one under par on the last hole (clue 1); Ms. Gold, who shot par (clue 3); and Beth and the owner of the green bag, both of whom shot over par, one scoring five on the hole (clue 6), and the other six (clue 2). Nether the under-par golfer (clue 1) nor Ms. Gold (clue 3) owns the gold bag, so Beth does. By clue 5, Ms. Black is one of the over-par players and is the owner of the green bag, while Helen shot par or under par. Helen is not Ms. Gold (clue 3), so she is the under-par golfer. By clue 4, Judy is Ms. Gold, and Helen owns the white golf bag. By elimination, Ms. Black is Sherrie, and Judy Gold's bag is black. Helen isn't Ms. White (clue 2), so Beth is, and Helen is Ms. Green. Beth White did not score six strokes (clue 2), so she scored five and Sherrie Black scored six. By clue 5, then, Helen's one-under-par score was three, so Judy Gold shot a par four. In sum:

> Helen Green, white, 3
> Judy Gold, black, 4
> Beth White, gold, 5
> Sherrie Black, green, 6

17.   LAST-MINUTE SHOPPERS

Mr. Barker was not the first or second customer waited on (clue 3), nor was Frye (clue 4). The first customer waited on was not Woodbury (clue 1) or Clark (clue 2), so was Schiller, a man, but not the man who bought batteries (clue 5). There are only two men mentioned, and Harold was not the first customer (clue 4), so he is Barker and bought batteries, while Schiller is Roy. The second customer wasn't Clark (clue 2), so was Woodbury. Harold Barker was not the last customer waited on (clue 4) so, by clue 3, the second customer was a woman who bought tape, Joan was the third, and Harold Barker was the fourth. By clue 4, Frye was the last customer waited on, and Joan bought flash cubes; since Frye did not buy ribbon, Roy Schiller did, and Frye was the customer who bought light bulbs. Joan's last name, by elimination, is Clark. Woodbury's first name is Marge (clue 2). By elimination, Frye's first name is Diana. In sum, in order waited on:

> Roy Schiller, ribbon
> Marge Woodbury, tape
> Joan Clark, flash cubes
> Harold Barker, batteries
> Diana Frye, light bulbs

18.   CONDO COMPLEX

By clue 3, the Kanes live two floors above the Hills, and Henry lives two floors above the Kanes. Henry's wife is Irma, and Dave Ellis lives on the floor just below them (clue 1). This spans five floors, which are either one through five or two through six. In either case, the Hills, who live on the first or second floor, are Mary and her husband John (clue 2). By clue 4, the only possibility is that these are floors one through five, Bob lives on the third floor, Sue and Mike on the second, and the Gordons on the sixth. Mr. Gordon, by elimination, is Frank. By clue 2, then, the Manns are on the second floor and are Sue and Mike, Ann is Bob's wife, and Donna is Dave's wife. By elimination, Frank's wife is Cathy, and Irma's and Henry's last name is Brooks. In sum:

> 1st   John and Mary Hill
> 2nd   Mike and Sue Mann
> 3rd   Bob and Ann Kane
> 4th   Dave and Donna Ellis
> 5th   Henry and Irma Brooks
> 6th   Frank and Cathy Gordon

19.   BARBERSHOP QUARTET

By clue 1, Jack, Wilson, and the stylist at the Hair Hut are, in some order, the second tenor, the baritone, and the bass. The stylist at the Hair Hut is not the bass (clue 4), nor is Wilson (clue 7); Jack is the bass. By clue 6, Tom and Meyers are the baritone and bass, so Tom is the baritone, while Meyers is Jack. The Hair Hut stylist is not Meyers or Wilson (clue 1), or Graham (clue 4); he is Dailey. The Daring-Do's stylist is neither Meyers (clue 3) nor Graham (clue 5); he is Wilson. By elimination, Graham is the tenor mentioned in clue 1. Dailey is not baritone Tom (clue 2); he is the second tenor. By elimination, Wilson is baritone Tom. Bill is not Graham (clue 9); Ray is and, by elimination, Bill is Dailey. Ray does not work at Comb & Co. (clue 8); he works at Bob's Barbershop while, by elimination, Jack Meyers works at Comb & Co. In summary:

> bass Jack Meyers, Comb & Co.
> baritone Tom Wilson, Daring-Do
> tenor Bill Dailey, Hair Hut
> tenor Ray Graham, Bob's Barbershop

20.   HOME-CARE WORKSHOP

Larry and Bette both attended the lawn-care and wallpapering classes, though not third (clue 5). By clue 3, Larry's last class wasn't about insulation, so it was kitchen remodeling. Each person took a different combination of classes, so Bette's last class was the one about insulation. By clue 1, Larry and Nina attended their first and third classes together, so she took kitchen remodeling last and either wallpapering or lawn care first. Clue 2 rules out lawn care. By clue 5 either Larry or Bette took lawn care first; so Nina and Larry took wallpapering first and Bette took lawn care first and wallpapering second (clue 5). Also by clue 5, Larry took lawn care second. Since Nina and Larry had different combinations of classes, Nina's second class was insulation, as was George's (clue 4). The only different combination of classes left for George is lawn care and kitchen remodeling. His third class was lawn care (clue 2) and his first was kitchen remodeling. In sum, in order of classes:

> Bette: lawn care, wallpapering, insulation
> George: kitchen remodeling, insulation, lawn care
> Larry: wallpapering, lawn care, kitchen remodeling
> Nina: wallpapering, insulation, kitchen remodeling

21. HOLIDAY CARDS

Carol's and Linda's were the last two cards (clue 1). By clue 3, then, Sue's card was third, Joe's card was second, and the first card was from Massachusetts. Carol's and Linda's husbands' names begin with the same letter (clue 1); since neither is married to Joe, it is the letter "B." The third card also had a "B" initial (clue 7); by elimination, the first card was from John. By clue 6, then, the Nye card was second and the Delaware card third. The husband who sent the fourth card isn't Bruce (clue 4), nor is he Bob (clue 5); by elimination, Bill sent the fourth card. Lucia and her husband sent one of the first two cards; the first card was from Massachusetts so, by clue 8, Lucia sent the second card from Vermont. By elimination, Sandy sent the first card. We've established the states of the first three cards, so, by clue 5, the Martin card was third, the Illinois card fourth, and Bob's card fifth. By elimination, Bruce sent the third card and the fifth card was from Pennsylvania. The Browns, by clue 4, sent the fifth card. By clue 2, Carol isn't from Pennsylvania, so Linda is, and Carol sent the fourth card. The Dales didn't send the first card (clue 3), so they sent the fourth card and, by elimination, the Warrens sent the first card. In sum, in the order in which the cards were opened:

> Sandy and John Warren, Massachusetts
> Lucia and Joe Nye, Vermont
> Sue and Bruce Martin, Delaware
> Carol and Bill Dale, Illinois
> Linda and Bob Brown, Pennsylvania

22. PICNIC IN THE PARK

Of the three generations, each woman has two daughters (clue 1), so each member of the younger two generations has a sister; Myrtle, then, is the grandmother (clue 8). No one is 11 (clue 9), so Iris, who is one year younger than her sister (clue 4), is not the sister of either Jasmine or her cousin Daphne, both of whom are 12 (clue 3). Iris, then, is in the middle generation, Rose, 10, and Violet, 9 (clue 4), and Iris is Lily's sister. By clue 5, Myrtle could not be 34 AND be the grandmother of 12-year-olds. If Lily were the 34-year-old, Iris would be 33, contradicting clue 9, so Iris is 34 and Lily is 35 (clue 4). Petunia, then, lives with Iris (clue 5). With only one dog per household, Daisy doesn't live with Iris or Lily (clue 2); Daisy lives with Myrtle, and Iris is Mrs. Meadows (also clue 2). By elimination, Pansy lives with Lily, but not with Jasmine (clue 6), so Daphne is Lily's daughter (clue 3), and Jasmine's mother is Iris. Daphne's sister is not 10 (clue 6), so she is 9-year-old Violet, and Jasmine's sister is 10-year-old Rose (clue 4). From clue 7, Lily is Mrs. Field, and Myrtle is Mrs. Flowers, who is 55. In summary:

> Myrtle Flowers (55) & Daisy
> Lily (35), Daphne (12), & Violet (9) Field & Pansy
> Iris (34), Jasmine (12), & Rose (10) Meadows & Petunia

23. TENNIS ROOKIES

Four of the seven new players are from the Hillcrest Club, and three from the Village Club. By clue 1, a man and a woman from each club are matched in the mixed doubles, with the remaining new players—two from Hillcrest and one from Village—entered in the women's singles, the men's doubles, and the men's singles. The one entered in the men's doubles, since his partner is not new, is John (clue 3). Those entered in the mixed doubles are then Dick Hutton and his partner (clue 2) and their opponents, Carl and his partner, whose last name is Spencer (clue 7). Jim Kent, by elimination, is entered in the men's singles. Mary Hill is not the one playing in the women's singles (clue 8); she is Dick Hutton's partner. By clue 4, Kate is entered in the women's singles and, since she and Jim play for the same club, that club is Hillcrest, while John plays for Village. Spencer's first name, by elimination, is Anita. By clue 5, Kate's last name is Marble, while Carl and Anita play for Village and Dick and Mary for Hillcrest. Tilden is John (clue 6); Carl's last name, by elimination, is Lopez. In sum:

> HILLCREST: Jim Kent, men's singles
> Kate Marble, women's singles
> Dick Hutton and Mary Hill, mixed doubles
>
> VILLAGE: John Tilden, men's doubles
> Carl Lopez and Anita Spencer, mixed doubles

24. HOME-TOWN REUNION

By clue 1, the five women are Ellen Johnson; the former Miss Bates, also now a Mrs. Johnson; a teacher who lives in Oregon; Sue; and the department-store buyer who, since she is hosting the reunion, still lives in Indiana. Only two West Coast states are mentioned, so by clue 2, the Oregon teacher is Cheryl, while the Realtor lives in California, and they are the only sisters mentioned, the Sanders sisters. Since neither Kay nor the former Miss Engle is married to one of the Johnson brothers (clue 4), Kay is the Indiana buyer, and Sue's maiden name was Engle. Ellen's sister-in-law, by elimination, is Judy. By elimination, Cheryl's sister, the California Realtor, is Ellen, and Kay's maiden name was Davis. Cheryl isn't Mrs. Owens (clues 2,3) or Mrs. Parker (clue 5); she is Mrs. Martin. Mrs. Parker isn't Kay (clue 5), so she is Sue and, since Mrs. Parker isn't a teacher, she is the computer programmer, while Judy is a teacher and Kay is Mrs. Owens. Sue lives in Pennsylvania and Judy in Maryland (clue 6). In sum:

> Ellen (Sanders) Johnson: realtor, Cal.
> Judy (Bates) Johnson: teacher, Md.
> Cheryl (Sanders) Martin: teacher, Ore.
> Kay (Davis) Owens: buyer, Ind.
> Sue (Engle) Parker: computer programmer, Pa.

25. BATON TWIRLERS' UNIFORMS

There are six baton twirlers, and no two twirlers had the same overall preference, so each voted for one of the six possible combinations—red hats with white blouses and blue skirts; red hats with blue blouses and white skirts; white hats with red blouses and blue skirts; white hats with blue blouses and red skirts; blue hats with red blouses and white skirts; and blue hats with white blouses and red skirts. By clue 2, Amanda voted for red hats. If she voted for white blouses and blue skirts, then, by clue 1, Cassie would also have voted for white blouses—and, since her overall preference was different from Amanda's, she would have voted for blue hats and red skirts. That, however, contradicts clue 4. So Amanda voted for blue blouses and white skirts, while Cassie voted for white hats, blue blouses, and red skirts. By clue 1, both Beverly and Dot voted for blue skirts; by elimination, the two who voted for blue hats were Elaine and Fran. Beverly voted for red hats and white blouses (clue 2), so Dot voted for white hats and red blouses. By clue 3, Elaine voted for red blouses and white skirts, so Fran voted for white blouses and red skirts. In sum:

	hats	blouses	skirts
Amanda	red	blue	white
Beverly	red	white	blue
Cassie	white	blue	red
Dot	white	red	blue
Elaine	blue	red	white
Fran	blue	white	red

26.   CHARITY DRIVE

Two men are mentioned, Mr. Nagler and Mr. Quinn, so they are Art and Jerry. Jerry isn't Mr. Nagler (clue 3), so Art is, and Jerry is Quinn. By clue 3, Darla's daycare center committee raised $500 more than Jerry Quinn's committee raised for kitchen equipment, which was in turn $500 more than Art Nagler's committee raised. Flora's committee then raised $500 less than Art's (clue 1). The most raised was $2500 and the least $500, so Jerry's committee raised at least $1500. $1500 was raised for bus service (clue 4); since all the figures were different, Jerry's committee raised more than $1500 for the kitchen equipment. Thus, Flora's committee raised more than $500, and the one whose committee raised the $500 is Ellie. Darla's committee raised the $2500 and, by the figures previously cited, Jerry's raised $2000, Art's $1500 for bus service, and Flora's $1000. By clue 1, the only way for the day camp to have raised $1000 more than the boys' club committee is if Darla raised the money for a day camp, and Art headed the boys' club committee (clue 1). Ellie headed the girls' club committee (clue 2). Flora didn't head the senior center committee (clue 1), so Jerry did, and Flora headed the park district committee. By clue 2, Ellie didn't raise money for the activity center, so Flora did, and Darla's name is Reed. Flora isn't Pace (clue 5), so Ellie is, and Flora is Oger. By elimination, Ellie raised money for art equipment. In sum:

$2500	Darla Reed	day care center, day camp
$2000	Jerry Quinn	senior center, kitchen equipment
$1500	Art Nagler	boys' club, bus service
$1000	Flora Oger	park district, activity center
$ 500	Ellie Pace	girls' club, art equipment

27.   FIVE GOLD RINGS

The rings were all different whole sizes. By clue 4, the ruby ring was size five, the ring Anna donated size seven, and the ring Tucker donated size eight. By clue 1, the jade ring was the smallest, and the ring Babs donated was smaller than size seven. Tucker's size-eight ring was then the largest. Toni's ring was neither the smallest (the jade) nor Tucker's largest ring (clue 6), so she donated the ruby. The largest ring donated wasn't the topaz (clue 2) or the emerald (clue 5); it was the sapphire. Since Ruth's ring wasn't the smallest (clue 3), she is Tucker and, by elimination, June donated the jade ring. By clue 5, the only way for the emerald ring to be smaller than Jacobs' ring is if Anna or Toni is Jacobs and Babs owns the emerald. By clue 3, Mandell's ring was a size 4; it was not Babs' emerald, so it was June's jade, and Babs' emerald was a size 6 (clue 1). By clue 5, then, Jacobs is Anna who, by elimination, donated the topaz ring. Toni isn't Warley (clue 6), so Babs is, and Toni's last name is Bremer. In sum:

June Mandell: jade, size four
Toni Bremer: ruby, size five
Babs Warley: emerald, size six
Anna Jacobs: topaz, size seven
Ruth Tucker: sapphire, size eight

28.   THE TUTORS

Each of the six tutors two subjects and each subject is handled by two of the six. Corelli's subjects are math and physics (clue 5). One of Vine's subjects is French (clue 3), and one of Evans' is chemistry (clue 6). A fourth person's subjects are English and French (clue 7). That person is not Adams (clue 2), Dalton (clue 4), or Vine (clue 7); Felton tutors English and French. The other English tutor is not Evans (clue 1), Dalton (clue 4), or Vine (clues 3, 7); Adams tutors English. By clue 8, neither Dalton nor Evans tutors history, so Adams and Vine do. Dalton doesn't tutor physics (clue 4), so Evans does and, by elimination, Dalton's subjects are math and chemistry. In sum:

Adams: English, history
Corelli: math, physics
Dalton: chemistry, math
Evans: chemistry, physics
Felton: English, French
Vine: French, history

29. UP, UP, AND AWAY!

The balloon that won the creativity award is not red (clue 2) or purple (clue 6), and does not belong to Flynn (clue 2) or Upton (clue 6), so it is either Adair's or Highland's. The gold balloon is neither Highland's (clue 3) nor Adair's (clue 7), so the balloon that won the creativity award is not gold; it is blue. The balloon that won the speed award is not purple (clue 1) or gold (clue 7); it is red. The owner of the red balloon is not Flynn (clue 2), Upton (clue 5), or Adair (clue 7), so Highland owns the red balloon, and Adair is the owner of the blue balloon that won for creativity. Denise's balloon is not purple or red (clue 1), or blue (clue 4), so it is gold. By clue 3, Craig is not Highland, so his balloon is not red, nor is it blue; it is purple. Denise's gold balloon did not win the beauty award (clue 4), so it won distance and, by elimination, Craig's purple balloon won the beauty award. Craig, therefore, is not Adair who owns the blue balloon; nor is Adair Ellen (clue 7), or Denise (clue 4); Adair is Fred. Highland, who owns the red balloon that won for speed, is not Denise (clue 1) or Craig (clue 3), so she is Ellen. Denise, who won for distance, is not Upton (clue 5), so she is Flynn and, by elimination, Craig is Upton. In summary:

> Fred Adair, blue, creativity of design
> Denise Flynn, gold, longest distance
> Ellen Highland, red, greatest speed
> Craig Upton, purple, beauty of design

30. 1950s FANTASY FILM FESTIVAL

"Ivanhoe," with Elizabeth Taylor (clue 8), was not shown the first week (clue 4) or the third (clue 7); it was shown the second week. It was not filmed in 1958 (clue 2), 1952 (clue 3), 1956 (clue 4), 1953 (clue 9), or 1959 (clue 12); it was filmed in 1951. It was directed by Richard Thorpe (clue 3) and also starred Robert Taylor (clue 11). "Safari" and the movie filmed in 1958 were shown the first week (clue 2). Janet Leigh starred in "Safari," which was filmed in 1956 (clue 4). It was not directed by Allan Dwan (clue 1), Kurt Neumann (clue 7), King Vidor (clue 10), or William Dieterle (clue 11); it was directed by Terence Young, and also starred Victor Mature (clue 5). The other first-week movie, filmed in 1958, was not directed by Kurt Neumann (clue 7), King Vidor (clue 10), or William Dieterle (clue 11); it was directed by Allan Dwan, and was "Enchanted Island" (clue 1). It did not star Piper Laurie (clue 7), Rita Hayworth (clue 9), or Gina Lollobrigida (clue 10); it starred Jane Powell, and also starred Dana Andrews (clue 6). "Ivanhoe" and the movie directed by William Dieterle were shown the second week (clue 11). Dieterle did not direct Piper Laurie (clue 7) or Gina Lollobrigida (clue 10); he directed Rita Hayworth in 1953 (clue 9). That movie was not "Son of Ali Baba" (clue 3) or "Solomon and Sheba" (clue 7); it was "Salome," and also starred Stewart Granger (clue 8). By elimination, "Solomon and Sheba" and "Son of Ali Baba" were shown the third week. "Solomon and Sheba" did not star Piper Laurie (clue 7); it starred Gina Lollobrigida, and was directed by King Vidor (clue 10). By elimination, Kurt Neumann directed "Son of Ali Baba," which was filmed in 1952 (clue 3) and, by elimination, starred Piper Laurie. Her co-star was not Yul Brynner (clue 12); he was Tony Curtis. By elimination, Yul Brynner starred in "Solomon and Sheba," which was made in 1959 (clue 12). In summary:

Week One:
"Enchanted Island" with Dana Andrews and Jane Powell, directed by Allan Dwan, 1958
"Safari" with Victor Mature and Janet Leigh, directed by Terence Young, 1956
Week Two:
"Ivanhoe" with Robert Taylor and Elizabeth Taylor, directed by Richard Thorpe, 1951
"Salome" with Stewart Granger and Rita Hayworth, directed by William Dieterle, 1953
Week Three:
"Solomon and Sheba" with Yul Brynner and Gina Lollobrigida, directed by King Vidor, 1959
"Son of Ali Baba" with Tony Curtis and Piper Laurie, directed by Kurt Neumann, 1952

31. JAMES BOMB, AGENT 000

Sixteen films were made in all, and the five actors starred in a different number of movies (clue 9). The only five different numbers that add up to sixteen are 1, 2, 3, 4, and 6. By clue

5, the first Bomb made six films and the "Zircons Are Forever" star made three. The first Bomb did not star in "Doctor Yes" (clue 1) or "Brassfinger" (clue 6); he starred in either "You Only Live Thrice" or "From Bulgaria With Love." By clue 1, Roger Bore made at least four films. He starred in neither "You Only Live Thrice" nor "From Bulgaria With Love" (clue 7), so he did not star in six; Roger Bore starred in four films, while Sean Corny and the "Doctor Yes" actor starred in one and two, in some order (clue 1). Roger Bore did not star in "Doctor Yes" (clue 1), "Zircons Are Forever" (clue 5), "From Bulgaria With Love," or "You Only Live Thrice" (clue 7); he starred in "Brassfinger." Timothy Dullthing starred in three films (clue 2), so he was the star of "Zircons Are Forever." George Lazyboy immediately preceded Roger Bore (clue 6), who immediately preceded Timothy Dullthing (clue 2). By clue 4, since Timothy made three films, he was not the fourth Bomb, and since Roger made four films he was not the second Bomb; George, then, was the third Bomb, Roger the fourth, and Timothy the fifth. Sean was not the first Bomb (clue 1); he was the second and, by elimination, David Never was the first. David starred in neither "Doctor Yes" (clue 1) nor "You Only Live Thrice" (clue 3); he starred in "From Bulgaria With Love." Sean Corny did not star in "Doctor Yes" (clue 1); he starred in "You Only Live Thrice" while, by elimination, George Lazyboy starred in "Doctor Yes." By clue 4, Sean Corny made two films so, by elimination, George Lazyboy made one. In summary:

> 1st: David Never, "From Bulgaria With Love," 6
> 2nd: Sean Corny, "You Only Live Thrice," 2
> 3rd: George Lazyboy, "Doctor Yes," 1
> 4th: Roger Bore, "Brassfinger," 4
> 5th: Timothy Dullthing, "Zircons Are Forever," 3

32. RECREATIONAL SPORTS

The friends ranged in age from twelve to eighteen, with no two the same age. The youngest, the twelve-year-old, is not Bill or Mary (clue 1), John (clue 2), or Tom (clue 3), so she is Jane. Tom is a year younger than Mary (clue 3), so Bill is at least two years younger than Mary (clue 1). By clue 1, Mary is at least sixteen. If Mary were sixteen then, by clue 3, Tom would be fifteen, and the hiker fourteen. By clue 1, Bill would be the hiker and Jane the golfer, leaving John to be the eighteen-year-old. John would then be the bowler (clue 2); however, this would contradict clue 4. The same holds true if Mary were seventeen. Mary, then, is eighteen, Tom is seventeen, and the hiker sixteen (clue 3). Since John is older than Bill (clue 2), the hiker is John. By clue 1, Bill is fifteen and Jane is the golfer. The bowler is then Tom (clue 2) and Mary is the swimmer (clue 4). Bill, by elimination, plays tennis. In sum, the friends and their sports, in order of age, are:

> Jane, 12—golf
> Bill, 15—tennis
> John, 16—hiking
> Tom, 17—bowling
> Mary, 18—swimming

33. CHINESE ZODIAC

Two of the girls are Mei Lin (clue 2) and Min Chi (clue 3). The Smith girl's event is the backstroke (clue 2). By clue 8, the Kent girl's event is diving. By clue 7, the Jones girl is competing for the first time and, as she was not born in the Year of the Rat, by clue 1, her event is the 100 yd. race. By clue 4, Lee's event is the 50 yd. race. By elimination, Min Chi and Mei Lin, not necessarily respectively, were in the breast stroke and 200 yd. events. By clue 9, Mei Lin's race was not the breast stroke so, by elimination, her event was 200 yds., and Min Chi's was the breast stroke. Also by elimination, Lee's surname is Wong. By clue 5, Sally's event was not 100 yds., so she is not Jones. Also by clue 5, she was born in the Year of the Monkey, so she is not Kent, who was born in the Year of the Horse (clue 8). By elimination, Sally is Smith. By clue 6, Mary was born in the Year of the Boar, so she is not Kent (clue 8); Mary is Jones, and Rose is Kent. Min Chi was born in the Year of the Sheep (clue 3). By clues 1 and 2, Mei Lin was not the one born in the Year of the Rat so, by elimination, she was born in the Year of the Dog, and Lee Wong in the Year of the Rat. Mei Lin was born in Honolulu (clue 2). Rose Kent was born in Denver (clue 3). Sally Smith was born in Boston (clue 5). Mary Jones was born in Hong Kong (clue 6). Lee was not born in Peking (clue 4) so, by elimination, she was born in Shanghai and Min Chi in Peking. In sum:

Min Chi	Peking	breast stroke	Sheep
Mary Jones	Hong Kong	100 yds.	Boar
Rose Kent	Denver	diving	Horse
Mei Lin	Honolulu	200 yds.	Dog
Sally Smith	Boston	backstroke	Monkey
Lee Wong	Shanghai	50 yds.	Rat

34. TELEPHONE LISTINGS

Since the names are alphabetized, the listings, from first to fifth are: Finnegan, Finneran, Fione, Fiore, Firster. By clue 4, the 271 number is Fione's. Also by clue 4, the 275 exchange is not listed last and, since neither Fione nor Firster is the physician, 275 is not the second or fourth listed exchange; 275 is Finnegan's exchange and the physician is Finneran. Since clue 2 mentions all five listings, physician Finneran's initials are T.U. The initials R.H. accompany a listing that is earlier than the minister's (clue 3), so the minister isn't Finnegan. So, by clue 2, Finnegan is in advertising and Firster is the minister. By clue 1, the 272 number is Finneran's, Fione is the orthodontist, and F.J. are Finnegan's initials. By elimination, Fiore is the one in insurance. By clue 5, the initials K.L. and the exchange 274 go with Fiore's listing. By elimination, Firster's telephone number begins with 273. By clue 3, Fione's initials are R.H. and Firster's are M.N. In sum:

> Finnegan, F.J., advertising, 275
> Finneran, T.U., physician, 272
> Fione, R.H., orthodontist, 271
> Fiore, K.L., insurance, 274
> Firster, M.N., minister, 273

35. THE TALLER, THE HEAVIER?

By clue 8, the shortest is between 60″ and 72″ tall, so the lightest is between 120 and 144 pounds. As they are 20 pounds apart (clue 1) and two of them weigh 150 and 170 pounds (clue 2), the weights are 130, 150, 170, and 190 pounds. By clue 8, again, the shortest is 65″, or 5′5″. The heights are two inches apart (clue 1), so the others are 5′7″, 5′9″, and 5′11″. Eric is not the lightest (clue 7) so, by clue 3, he weighs 150, the French major 170, and the English major 190. The English major is Peck, and the chemistry major weighs 130 (clue 4). Eric, by elimination, is the math major. English major Peck is taller than at least two others (clue 5). By clue 6, then, Finn is also one of the two tallest, math major Eric is second shortest at 5′7″, and Harry is the shortest at 5′5″. Eric isn't Vogel, (clue 7), so he is Stone, and Harry is Vogel. By clue 5, English major Peck is tallest; Gary is Finn and is 5′9″. Peck is Jeff. Eric weighs 150 so, by clue 2, Harry is the 170-pound French major.
By elimination, Gary Finn is the chemistry major. In sum:

> Gary Finn, chemistry: 130 lbs., 5′9″
> Jeff Peck, English: 190 lbs., 5′11″
> Eric Stone, math: 150 lbs., 5′7″
> Harry Vogel, French: 170 lbs., 5′5″

36. BALANCING SEESAWS

The eight children are Jane, the Jefferson boy, a second girl who weighed 45 pounds (clue 2), two Jackson boys, a fourth boy, and the Johnson twins (clue 3). The twins, then, are girls; neither is Jane (clue 2). Since they weighed 60 pounds each (clue 3), neither is Jenny (clues 4 and 6); they are Janis and Joy. Since five children shared two seesaws (clue 3), two children were on one of these and three on the other. If Janis and Joy did not share a seesaw, one would have been riding with only one other person who would have weighed 60 pounds in order for the seesaw to balance. This contradicts clue 3, so Janis and Joy Johnson shared a seesaw, as did the Jackson boys and Jenny's brother. By elimination, Jenny was the girl who weighed 45 pounds. The Jenkins girl's weight was an even number (clue 4). Since Jenny weighed 45 pounds, Jane is the Jenkins girl. By elimination, Jenny's surname is Jones, as is her brother's on the last seesaw. Since the Jones boy was the lightest on his seesaw (clue 3), he was on the same side as one of the Jackson brothers. Jeff weighed 50 pounds (clue 5), so he is not the Jefferson boy (since Jane Jenkins would then have weighed 95 pounds, which is not an even number). Jeff was one of the boys on the last seesaw. The last of these boys was Joe, who weighed 90 pounds (clue 4). In order for the last seesaw to balance, one boy weighed 40 pounds, so he is the Jones boy (clue 3). Joe is Jackson, then, and his brother is Jeff. If John were Jefferson, he would have weighed 45 pounds (clue 4), which would contradict clue 3. Jim, then, is Jefferson, and John is the Jones boy who weighed 40 pounds. Jane weighed 80 (clue 4) and Jim weighed 35. In sum:

> First seesaw: Jane Jenkins, 80 pounds, with
> Jenny Jones, 45 pounds and
> Jim Jefferson, 35 pounds
> Second seesaw: Janis Johnson, 60 pounds, with
> Joy Johnson, 60 pounds
> Third seesaw: Joe Jackson, 90 pounds, with
> Jeff Jackson, 50 pounds and
> John Jones, 40 pounds

37. SPECIALTIES

Ann has the office in the southeast corner of the building (clue 6). By clue 7, offices 310 and 340, as well as 320 and 330, are diagonally across from each other. Winter, then, who is next to the internist and diagonally across from 310 (clue 4), has office 340. Miller's office and office 330 are, in some order, the northeast and northwest offices (clue 3). If 330 were the northeast office, Miller would be in the northwest office, which would be 310. Ann, then, would have office 340 and be Winter. The pediatrician is next to Ann, but not in 330 (clue 1), so would be in 320. This, however, would contradict clue 2, since Cline, who is not in 320, would, by elimination, be in 330, which is diagonally across from the pediatrician, not the surgeon. Office 330 is, then, the northwest office; Miller is in the northeast office; and Ann is in 320. Winter, in 340, is in the southwest office, and Miller, by elimination, is in 310. Margaret, by clue 5, has the southwest office and is Winter. The pediatrician, who is male and has an offce next to Ann (clue 1), is Miller. By clue 2, Cline is not Ann in 320, so Cline is in 330 and Ann is the surgeon. By elimination, Ann is Spencer. The internist, who is next to Margaret Winter, is Cline. He is not John (clue 4), so Miller is John. By elimination, Cline is Richard, while Winter is the allergist. In sum:

> Richard Cline, internist, 330
> John Miller, pediatrician, 310
> Ann Spencer, surgeon, 320
> Margaret Winter, allergist, 340

38. BUSY MORNING

No two women did the same three chores in the same order. The women who washed their hair did it last (clue 3) and cleaned house first (clue 1); there were, then, two of them, and one went to the library second, the other to the bank. By clue 1, there are precisely four possibilities left for the other four women: Two cleaned house first, and one of these went to the bank next and then to the library, while the other reversed those errands, while the remaining two cleaned house last, and one went first to the bank and then to the library, the other first to the library and then to the bank. The building is 22 stories tall. By clue 4, none of the six lives on the fifth floor or lower than the fourth so, by clue 2, Flo lives on the fourth, the woman who went to the library first lives on the eighth, and Ms. Nelson lives on the 16th, the highest. Ms. Nelson is the one who went to the bank last (clue 9). The two lowest of the three consecutive floors are those of the women who washed their hair (clue 5); they are not above the eighth (clue 7), so they are the sixth and seventh. None of the six lives on the twelfth floor (clue 4) so, by clue 7, Joan lives on the 14th floor and is the one who went to the bank first (clue 6). Like her, the seventh-floor woman went to the library second (clue 7), so the sixth-floor woman went to the bank second. By elimination, Flo is the woman in clue 8 who went to the library last. Also by clue 8, Ann lives on the sixth floor and Ms. Kraft on the eighth. By clue 6, Ann is Ms. Briggs and Ms. Kraft is Connie. The only floor for Grace

147

Elmont is the seventh, so Joan is Ms. Duncan (clue 10). By elimination, Flo is Ms. Hanks and Ms. Nelson is Mary. In sum:

4, Flo Hanks: cleaning, bank, library
6, Ann Briggs: cleaning, bank, shampoo
7, Grace Elmont: cleaning, library, shampoo
8, Connie Kraft: library, bank, cleaning
14, Joan Duncan: bank, library, cleaning
16, Mary Nelson: cleaning, library, bank

39. HERITAGE MALL

Ms. Gallagher's store is on the north side (clue 5) and upper level (clue 7), so hers is either 5 or 6, and the store offering the keychains is store 1 or 2 (clue 7). The store with keychains is on the west side (clue 9), so it is store 1, and Ms. Gallagher's is store 5 (clue 7). Mr. Chadwick's store is on the lower level (clue 1) west side (clue 9), so his is store 3 and the book and card stores are, in some order, stores 5 and 7 (also clue 9). The card shop is not store 5 (clue 4); it is store 7, and the lapel pins were passed out in store 3 (clue 4). By elimination, store 5 is the book store. The pet store is not store 1, 2, 3, or 4 (clue 6), or store 6 (clue 3); it is store 8. By clue 3, Mr. Chadwick's store 3 which gave out lapel pins is the record store. By clue 6, Ms. Gallagher's store 5 passed out memo pads, and Ms. Duncan and Ms. Jacobson own, in some order, stores 6 and 7. So, by clue 3, Ms. Nicholas' store was store 4 and store 7 passed out pocket calendars. The pet store, store 8, did not pass out seed packets (clue 1), rulers, or magnets (clue 5); it passed out balloons. It is not owned by Mr. Fleming (clue 1) or Mr. Westcott (clue 8); it is owned by Mr. Meyer. Mr. Westcott therefore owns store 2 (clue 8) and, by elimination, Mr. Fleming owns store 1. Store 4 did not pass out the ruler or magnet (clue 5); it passed out the seed packets. The clothes store is store 2 (clue 1). Mr. Westcott's store did not pass out the magnet (clue 8); it passed out the ruler. By elimination, store 6 passed out the magnet. By clue 8, store 6 is not the toy store, so the toy store is store 4. The shoe store is not store 6 that gave out the magnet (clue 5); it is store 1. By elimination, store 6 is the fabric shop. It is not owned by Ms. Jacobson (clue 2); it is owned by Ms. Duncan and, by elimination, Ms. Jacobson owns store 7. In summary:

1. Mr. Fleming's shoe store—keychains
2. Mr. Westcott's clothes store—rulers
3. Mr. Chadwick's record store—lapel pins
4. Ms. Nicholas' toy store—seed packets
5. Ms. Gallagher's book store—memo pads
6. Ms. Duncan's fabric shop—magnets
7. Ms. Jacobson's card shop—pocket calendars
8. Mr. Meyer's pet store—balloons

40. DOUGHNUTS

The two who ordered black coffee with no sugar (clue 1) are not Workman (clue 2), Quiller (clue 5), or Cox (clue 6); they are Fuller and Parker. Neither usually orders a bear claw (clue 1), cheese Danish (clue 2), or cinnamon twist (clue 6), nor did either order a bran muffin or cinnamon roll last week (clues 1, 5); Parker has never ordered a Danish (clue 7), so Parker usually orders a maple bar, and Fuller usually orders a raspberry Danish. Fuller, then, is not Carol (clue 3), Bert (clue 4), Jeremy or Roger (clues 1, 2); Lila is Fuller, whose order last week was not a prune Danish (clue 3) or a blueberry muffin (clue 4), so was an apple fritter. Parker didn't order a prune Danish last week (clue 7), so ordered a blueberry muffin. Parker, then, isn't Bert (clue 4), Jeremy or Roger (clues 1, 2); she is Carol. Jeremy doesn't usually order a bear claw (clue 1); he doesn't use sugar in his coffee (clue 8), so he doesn't usually order a cinnamon twist (clue 6); Jeremy usually orders a cheese Danish, and the one who ordered a bran muffin last week usually orders a cinnamon twist (clues 1, 6). Workman doesn't usually order a cheese Danish (clue 2), so Jeremy isn't Workman or Cox (clues 6, 8); Jeremy is Quiller, who ordered coffee with cream (clue 5). Jeremy didn't order a cinnamon roll last week (also clue 5), so he ordered a prune Danish. Roger is not Workman (clue 2), so Roger is Cox and Bert is Workman. Roger doesn't usually order a cinnamon twist (clue 6), so Bert does. Roger Cox, then, usually orders a bear claw, but ordered a cinnamon roll last week, and ordered both cream and sugar in his coffee (clues 5, 6), while Workman ordered sugar in his coffee (clue 6). In summary, with usual orders in parentheses:

Roger Cox, coffee with cream & sugar, cinnamon roll (bear claw)
Lila Fuller, black coffee, apple fritter (raspberry Danish)
Carol Parker, black coffee, blueberry muffin (maple bar)
Jeremy Quiller, coffee with cream, prune Danish (cheese Danish)
Bert Workman, coffee with sugar, bran muffin (cinnamon twist)

41.   THE COLTS

By clue 1, each of three stallions—Commendation, Dooby Do, and Spectacular—sired two of the six colts. By clue 3, none of the four mares is the mother of more than two of the six. Two of the colts are the offspring of Dooby Do and the mare named Clockbreaker (clue 7), so these two are the *only* offspring of this sire and dam and are not related to any of the other colts. By clue 2, Go For It and High Falutin have the same sire. Thus, High Falutin's kinship with Lucky Fellow (clue 4) is that they have the same dam, but they have different sires. By clue 5, Lucky Fellow is also related to Catch Me Now, so the kinship of these two is that of having the same sire but different dams; by the same clue, that sire is not Commendation and so is Spectacular, while the sire of Go For It and High Falutin is Commendation. The two offspring of Dooby Do and Clockbreaker are Mercury's Boy and Quicksilver. By clue 8, Heights of Glory is not the mother of Go For It, but does have a colt by Commendation; that colt is High Falutin. Thus, Heights of Glory is also the dam of Lucky Fellow. Fabulous has at least one colt by Spectacular (clue 6), so that colt is Catch Me Now. By elimination, Hob Nob is the mother of Go For It. In sum, with the name of the dam listed first:

Catch Me Now: Fabulous, Spectacular
Go For It: Hob Nob, Commendation
High Falutin: Heights of Glory, Commendation
Lucky Fellow: Heights of Glory, Spectacular
Mercury's Boy: Clockbreaker, Dooby Do
Quicksilver: Clockbreaker, Dooby Do

42.   NEW SUITS

By clue 8, these four suits were purchased in consecutive order: a green one, the one Charles bought, the one that Donovan bought, and a suit that cost $150; a brown suit was purchased earlier than any of these (clue 2). Clue 5 also describes three consecutive purchases—a gray suit, Anthony's, and Miller's; since there are six altogether, this sequence must overlap that described in clue 8. If the gray suit were the first one purchased and Anthony's the second, with Miller buying the green suit mentioned in clue 8, Anthony would have bought the brown suit, contradicting clue 1. If the gray suit were Donovan's purchase, Miller's would be the last of the six purchases, contradicting clue 5. Charles did not buy the gray suit (clue 9). The gray suit, then, was the second one purchased, Anthony's was the third purchase and was a green suit, Charles is Miller and made the fourth purchase, Donovan made the fifth purchase, and a suit that cost $150 was the last one bought; the brown suit was the first purchase. By clue 3, Larry made the second purchase and Carter the first. Anthony isn't Akins (clue 10) so, by clue 11, Akins' purchase—which was the navy suit—was the last one, and Larry's suit cost $300. Larry isn't Landman (clue 10), so Anthony is, and Larry's last name is Brant. David isn't Donovan (clue 10) and, by clue 4, he isn't Akins, so he is Carter and his suit cost $250. By clue 6, Matt is Akins, and Donovan's suit cost $200. Donovan, by elimination, is Burt. Charles's suit cost $100 (clue 12). All five prices established thus far are different so, by clue 7, Anthony paid the same price Matt did, $150. By clue 9, Charles Miller bought the second green suit and Burt Donovan the black one. In sum, in order of purchase:

David Carter: brown, $250
Larry Brant: gray, $300
Anthony Landman: green, $150
Charles Miller: green, $100
Burt Donovan: black, $200
Matt Akins: navy, $150

43.   SWEET MIX

Since there were more than twice as many vanilla nuggets as Heidi's candies (clue 1), there were either thirteen or sixteen nuggets and Heidi chose either five or six. Heidi did not choose the raspberry rolls (clue 1) or butter ribbons (clue 5). Since there were more than six of each, she didn't choose fudge fingers (clue 2), or choco-caramels (clue 4); she chose the cinnamon squares. By clue 3, Heidi chose six and Becky chose five. For the same reasons as Heidi, Becky did not choose vanilla nuggets, fudge fingers, or choco-caramels, nor did she choose the butter ribbons (clue 3); she chose the raspberry rolls. There were at least thirteen vanilla nuggets (clue 1) and, by clue 2, there were also at least thirteen fudge fingers. By clues 4 and 7, then, there were ten choco-caramels, Louise chose eight candies, Montgomery six and Hines five. Hines is Becky and Montgomery is Heidi. By elimination, there were eight butter ribbons, so they were Louise's choice. By clue 2, Darren chose the ten choco-caramels, Sullivan chose thirteen, and there were sixteen fudge fingers. By elimination, Sullivan chose thirteen vanilla nuggets. Sullivan is not Tom (clue 6), so he's Walter and, by elimination, Tom chose sixteen fudge fingers. Louise is neither Coleman (clue 5) nor Farley (clue 8); she is Wolfe. Farley did not choose the fudge fingers (clue 8), so he is Darren and Coleman is Tom. In sum:

> Becky Hines, raspberry rolls, five
> Darren Farley, choco-caramels, ten
> Heidi Montgomery, cinnamon squares, six
> Louise Wolfe, butter ribbons, eight
> Tom Coleman, fudge fingers, sixteen
> Walter Sullivan, vanilla nuggets, thirteen

44.   HOW MANY CANDLES?

By clue 4, Jill is eight years old, the Ramsey child is ten, and the child who wore the blue hat is eleven. One child, who is not Lynn, is nine (clue 7). By clue 1, then, Lynn is the eleven-year-old, and Chuck is nine. By clues 3 and 5, which mention three last names, there are two pairs of children who are the same age; these are the eight- and ten-year-olds (clue 1). One of the ten-year-olds is the Ramsey child, so clue 5 refers to the eight-year-olds. By clue 3, then, the Ramsey child is Adam, and the other ten-year-old is the Baker child. The latter is Randy, and Chuck wore the green hat (clue 6). By elimination, the second eight-year-old is Cindy. Jill's hat was purple (clue 9). By clue 5, Jill's last name is Harris and Cindy's is March. The Foster child is Chuck, and Cindy wore the pink hat (clue 2). Lynn, by elimination, is the Cummings child. Adam's hat wasn't yellow (clue 8), so Randy's was, and Adam, by elimination, was the birthday child who wore the orange hat (clue 10); since Adam is ten years old, the cake had eleven candles. In sum:

> Randy Baker, yellow, 10
> Lynn Cummings, blue, 11
> Chuck Foster, green, 9
> Jill Harris, purple, 8
> Cindy March, pink, 8
> Adam Ramsey, orange, 10 (eleven candles on his cake)

45.   BARGAIN BONANZA

Two of the six are Jason, who sold a set of tires for $60, and O'Keefe, who bought a radio (clue 2). Two others are Bellamy, who sold a dryer for $50, and Ava, who bought the dryer and sold a $20 item (clue 4). Ms. Heston, a fifth, bought the tires from Jason and sold a $40 item (clue 3). The sixth person is the one who bought the crib and sold a bike for $25 (clue 1). By clue 5, Dan, who sold a TV to Reid, is O'Keefe, and Reid, who bought it, is Jason; since Jason received $15 more than he spent, the TV cost him $45. Bellamy, by elimination, bought the bike. Dixie, who bought Ms. Heston's $40 item (clue 3), was the purchaser of the crib; since she isn't Firth (clue 3), she is Cox, and Ava is Firth. By elimination, the $20 item Ava sold was the radio Dan bought; Ms. Heston is Lisa; and Bellamy is Sam. In sum:

> Sam Bellamy: sold $50 dryer, bought $25 bike
> Dixie Cox: sold $25 bike, bought $40 crib

Ava Firth: sold $20 radio, bought $50 dryer
Lisa Heston: sold $40 crib, bought $60 tires
Dan O'Keefe: sold $45 TV, bought $20 radio
Jason Reid: sold $60 tires, bought $45 TV

46. DIET DELIGHTS

One woman lost 18 pounds and another 12 (clue 4). The zoologist lost 8 pounds (clue 8) and Ms. Andrews the least, 7 pounds (clue 5). These four losses add up to 45 pounds; since the six lost a total of 70 pounds, the two other weights equal 25 pounds. Mary, who lost the most weight, lost 8 pounds more than the accountant (clue 1). There are no 8-pound differences between any two weight losses already known, so either Mary's or the accountant's (or both) must be the missing weight(s). Mary's weight loss, however, cannot be more than 18 pounds, since then the sixth weight loss would be 6 or fewer pounds (25 minus 19). Thus, the 18-pound weight loss was Mary's, and the accountant lost 10 pounds; the remaining woman lost 15 pounds (25 minus 10). Mary lost 18 pounds, a second woman 15, a third 12, the accountant 10, the zoologist 8, and Ms. Andrews 7. By clue 4, Mary is a lawyer, and the 12-pound loss was Anne's. There are only 2 sets of weights that differ by 5 pounds (15 and 10; 12 and 7). Since the accountant lost 10 pounds, by clue 9, Ms. Andrews is the saleswoman and Anne's last name is Taylor. The 15-pound loss was Ms. Johnson's, and the accountant is Nancy (clue 2). Sarah Nelson (clue 7) is the zoologist. Photographer Trudy (clue 3) is Ms. Johnson. Anne Taylor is a musician, and Mary's last name is Stevens (clue 6). By elimination, Nancy's surname is Martin, and Ms. Andrews' first name is Janet. In sum:

> Mary Stevens, lawyer: 18 lbs.
> Trudy Johnson, photographer: 15 lbs.
> Anne Taylor, musician: 12 lbs.
> Nancy Martin, accountant: 10 lbs.
> Sarah Nelson, zoologist: 8 lbs.
> Janet Andrews, saleswoman: 7 lbs.

47. FLOWERING TREES

No one could have had four right, since then the fifth answer would have been correct as well. By clue 4, each child got a different number correct, so one had all five right, and the others had three, two, one and zero right. Joe had all five right (clue 4), and the correct answers are: elm, #1; magnolia, #2; cherry, #3; horse-chestnut, #4; and linden, #5 (clue 6). Also by clue 4, the child with three right marked the horse-chestnut #4, Ellen had two right, the child with one right marked the cherry #3, and the Gregg child had all wrong. These last two children could not have had the elm and the linden correct, so, by clue 3, they marked them #2 and #4 respectively, while the other three children each marked them correctly, #1 and #5 respectively. Mary, then, who thought the cherry was #5 (clue 1), is the Gregg child. The child with three right answers gave the magnolia #3 and the cherry #2. By clue 5, since the horse-chestnut was #4 and Mary had no correct answers, Joe is the Brown child, and Don the one who had three correct answers. The one who had one right, by elimination, is Laura. Mary did not give the horse-chestnut #1 (clue 5), so Laura did and Mary made that #3. By clue 5, Ellen is the Clark child; she, like Mary, gave the horse-chestnut #3. By elimination, the magnolia was called #5 by Laura and #1 by Mary. Ellen was right only on the elm and linden, so she said the magnolia was #4 and the cherry #2. Don is not the Fox child (clue 2), so Laura is and Don's last name is Andrews. In sum:

all right:	Joe Brown	elm	mag.	cherry	hor.-ch,	lin.
3 right:	Don Andrews	elm	cherry	mag.	hor.-ch.	lin.
2 right:	Ellen Clark	elm	cherry	hor.-ch.	mag.	lin.
1 right:	Laura Fox	hor.-ch.	elm	cherry	lin.	mag.
0 right:	Mary Gregg	mag	elm.	hor.-ch	lin.	cherry

48. AT THE AUCTION

There are three men among the five. Jonathan spent the least (clue 5). Joseph spent $5,000 less than the man from Rome (clue 3), so the man from Rome is Daniel. The man from

Beverly Hills, who paid twice as much for jewelry as did Maria from London (clue 1) is Joseph. Helena didn't make the most expensive purchase (clue 6), so Daniel did. Since the clock cost less than Helena's purchase (clue 6), and Daniel didn't buy the tea service (clue 3), he bought the painting; Jonathan bought the clock and Helena the tea service. Helena's tea service cost $15,000 (clue 6) so, by clue 3, Joseph spent $20,000, and Daniel's painting cost $25,000. Maria spent $10,000 (clue 1). Helena's last name is Graystone (clue 2). By clue 7, Bandervilt is Maria, and Jonathan is from New York and spent $5,000; Helena, by elimination, is from Paris. By clue 4, La Mar is neither Daniel nor Jonathan, so he is Joseph and must have bought the ring, while Maria bought the necklace. Vesterhouse isn't from New York (clue 7), so he is Daniel, and Jonathan's last name is Barrington. In sum:

> Daniel Vesterhouse, Rome: $25,000 painting
> Joseph LaMar, Beverly Hills: $20,000 ring
> Helena Graystone, Paris: $15,000 tea service
> Maria Bandervilt, London: $10,000 necklace
> Jonathan Barrington, New York: $5,000 clock

49. DESIGNER MUGS

The mug in position one is not Ambrose's (clue 1), Giselle's (clue 2), Florian's (clue 3), Brendan's (clue 4) or Renata's (clue 5); it is Zandra's. The mug in position six is not "Chipmunk" (clue 1), "Scenic" (clue 2), "Touchdown" (clue 3), "Owl" (clue 4), or "Poppy" (clue 5); it is "Butterfly." Renata's mug is to the right of "Poppy" (clue 5) and to the left of "Chipmunk" (clue 9); "Chipmunk" is to the left of Ambrose's mug (clue 1) which was not "Butterfly" (clue 8). Since Zandra in the first position did not design "Poppy" (clue 7), and Ambrose did not design "Butterfly" (clue 8), "Poppy" is in four, Renata's is in two, "Chipmunk" is in five, and Ambrose's is in three. Florian's mug is in the bottom row, but not in six (clue 3), or four (clue 7); it is in five. Giselle's mug costs more than Renata's (clue 2), which is more than a Florian's "Chipmunk" (clue 5), which is more than Brendan's, which is not the least expensive (clue 9), so Giselle's costs at least $9.50. "Butterfly" costs less than $9.50 (clue 10), so Giselle's mug is not in six; it is in four, and, by elimination, Brendan's is in six. "Scenic" is in one (clue 2). Ambrose's mug is not "Owl" (clue 1), so it is "Touchdown" and Renata's is "Owl." Giselle's mug also costs more than Zandra's "Scenic Farm" (clue 6), so Giselle's costs $10. Renata's also costs more than Zandra's, so Renata's mug costs $9.50. Since Florian's costs less than Zandra's (clue 10), Zandra's costs $8.50. Florians costs more than Brendan's (clue 10), and Brendan's was not the least expensive (clue 9), so Florian's costs $8, and Brendan's costs $7.50, while, by elimination, Ambrose's cost $6. In summary:

> 1. Zandra, "Scenic Farm," $8.50
> 2. Renata, "Owl Family," $9.50
> 3. Ambrose, "Touchdown!", $6
> 4. Giselle, "Poppy Serenade," $10
> 5. Florian, "Chipmunk Chase," $8
> 6. Brendan, "Butterfly Fantasy," $7.50

50. BLOOMIN' GRANDKIDS

Square three is not Tim's (clue 1), Greg's (clue 2), Dawn's (clue 4), Cindy's (clue 5), Luci's (clue 6), or Andy's (clue 7). Since the violet is not in square three (clue 3), square three is not Kristy's (clue 1). Tim's square is directly under the violet and to the left of Dawn's (clue 9) which is to the left of the petunia (clue 4), which puts Tim's and the violet's squares in the first column. Toby's is directly to the right of the violet (clue 3), so his square is either two or five. By elimination, square three is Ryan's. The flower in Ryan's square has four letters (clue 1), but is not the rose (clue 3); it is the iris. Cindy's square is six (clue 5). If Toby's square were square two, the violet would be in one (clue 3) and the rose in five (clue 3). Tim's square would be four (clue 9) and Dawn's would be five (clues 4, 9). Luci's square would be one (clue 6) and the marigold would be in four (clue 6). Andy's square would be nine (clue 7) and the daffodil would be in six (clue 7). The petunia would be nine (clue 4). Square seven would be Greg's (clue 8), which would leave no corner for the daisy (clue 8). Toby's square, then, is not two; it is square five. By clue 3, the violet is in square four and the rose is in eight. Tim's square is seven (clue 9). Since Dawn's square is left of the petunia (clue 4), hers is eight (clue 9). Greg's square is not one (clue 2), so it is nine (clue 8). The tulip is in six (clue 2). The petunia is then in nine (clue 4). Andy's square is four (clue 7). By clue 6, Luci's square is two, and the marigold is five. By elimination, Kristy's is one. The daffodil is in one (clue 7). The daisy is in seven (clue 8) and, by elimination, the pansy is in two. In summary:

Kristy daffodil	Luci pansy	Ryan iris
Andy violet	Toby marigold	Cindy tulip
Tim daisy	Dawn rose	Greg petunia

51. STUDENTS' SCHEDULES

By clue 1, no two of the six students have the same schedule: two attend evening classes, one working mornings and studying afternoons and the other the reverse; two work in the evenings, one attending morning classes and studying in the afternoon, the other the reverse; and the other two study in the evening, one working mornings and attending classes in the afternoon, the other the reverse. Kathy and Price are the two who have evening classes (clue 2); by clue 6, Kathy works afternoons and studies in the morning, so Price works mornings and studies in the afternoon. The two who work in the evening are Collins and Nancy (clue 4). Ingalls, like Price, works mornings (clue 2) and so has afternoon classes and studies in the evening. Mark and Christine study at the same time (clue 5), so that is either afternoons or evenings. If it were afternoons, they would be (not necessarily respectively) Price and Collins. Then Steve, who has no afternoon classes (clue 5) and therefore isn't Ingalls, would be the sixth student, studying in the evening and working afternoons, when Price and Collins were the two studying. This, however, would contradict clue 5. Therefore, Mark and Christine study evenings and are in some order Ingalls and the sixth student. Louis isn't Collins (clues 3, 4), so he is Price, and Collins is Steve. Steve Collins works evenings; by clue 5, he attends classes mornings and studies afternoons, and Walton is the one who, like Ingalls, studies evenings; Walton attends morning classes and works afternoons. Nancy, who studies mornings and attends afternoon classes, isn't Mason (clue 4); she is Baker, while Mason is Kathy. By clue 5, then, Mark works mornings while Baker studies, so he is Ingalls, and Walton is Christine. In sum:

	Morning	*Afternoon*	*Evening*
Nancy Baker	Study	Classes	Work
Steve Collins	Classes	Study	Work
Mark Ingalls	Work	Classes	Study
Kathy Mason	Study	Work	Classes
Louis Price	Work	Study	Classes
Christine Walton	Classes	Work	Study

52. VALENTINE'S DAY PARTY

Each girl brought a gift for a boy and vice versa (clue 2), so there were three of each in the group. By clue 5, no two children exchanged gifts. Let us explore the gift-giving pattern this way: A girl, we'll call "A," gave a gift to a boy, we'll designate "B." Since "B" didn't give a gift in return to "A," he gave his gift to a second girl; we'll call her "C." Since she then did not give her gift to "B," a fourth child (a second boy) enters the picture, and we'll call him "D." Now, "D" didn't give his gift to "C"; and if he gave his gift to "A," that would leave the two remaining children exchanging gifts, contradicting clue 5, so "D" must have given his gift to the third girl, whom we'll call "E." She, in turn, can only have given her gift to the remaining boy, whom we can designate "F," and he can only have given his gift to the girl we called "A." There were three edible gifts (the cupcake, the bag of peanuts, and the candy bar) and three others (the Valentine card, the paper flower, and the birthday card). Let's call Jane child "A," since she is the only one who didn't give or receive something edible (clue 11). That means that she received the flower or one of the cards from boy "F," and she gave the flower or one of the cards to boy "B." Since every other child gave and/or received something edible, boy "F" received something edible from girl "E," and boy "B" gave something edible to girl "C." Lee, who gave a boy a birthday card (clue 6), can only be girl "C," and the boy who received the birthday card is boy "D." By elimination, boy "D's" gift to girl "E" was something edible, and girl "E" is Barbara. There is only one child, then, who both gave and received something to eat—girl "E," Barbara; by clue 10, her last name is Ross. Jane received a paper gift, so the Adams girl, who received a candy bar (clue 8), must be Lee; Jane is the Carlson girl, at whose home the party was held. The birthday boy, boy "D," didn't bring Barbara Ross peanuts (clue 12); he brought her the cupcake, and the peanuts were Barbara's gift to boy "F." One gift, the most expensive, cost 30¢ (clue 1). Three of the gifts were bought and three homemade, including the paper flower (clue 3). Clue 4 mentions all purchased gifts. The peanuts were bought but did not cost the most. If the gift Mike brought had cost 30¢, that would put a price of 40¢ on the one he received. So it was the gift Mike received which cost 30¢, the one he bought cost 25¢, and the peanuts cost 15¢. The last name of boy "F," to whom Barbara gave the peanuts, isn't Burns (clue 7) or Green (clue 9), so it is Dobbs. The Green child in clue 9, who received and gave a homemade gift, is not boy "B" who gave Lee Adams the candy bar, which was a brand name and thus was purchased (clue 8), so the Green child is boy "D," who received the birthday card and gave the cupcake. Mike, who received the 30¢ gift, is not Dobbs, so he is boy "B," and his last name, by elimination, is Burns; the gift he received from Jane must have been the Valentine card, while the homemade paper flower was Jane's gift from the Dobbs boy. The candy bar then cost 25¢. By clue 12, the Green boy is Pat, and Kit is the Dobbs boy. In sum:

> Jane Carlson gave 30¢ Valentine card to
> Mike Burns, who gave 25¢ candy bar to
> Lee Adams, who gave homemade birthday card to
> Pat Green, who gave homemade cupcake to
> Barbara Ross, who gave 15¢ bag of peanuts to
> Kit Dobbs, who gave homemade paper flower to Jane

53.   SEAT SWITCH

By clue 2, the boys with the end seats before the switch each had the last initial P. The Bell boy, to move three seats to his right (clue 6) must have begun in the second seat from the left and switched to the end seat on the right. By clue 3, then, the Parton boy had the left end seat and Jerry the seat next to him after the switch. Two boys moved more than one seat away from their first seats (clue 4). We now know one is Bell and the other Parton, since he didn't begin in the first two seats. By clue 1, Mike is Bell and the Parton boy began in the third seat from the left. Since boys with the same initials had the original end seats (clue 2), they are Jerry and John, whose last names are Parker and Penn, in some order. Jerry, by clue 4, had the left end seat before the switch and John the right. The Gallo boy, by elimination, started in the fourth seat from the left. By clue 5, Frank sat just to the left of the Penn boy before and after the switch. Jerry, Mike, and the Parton boy began in the first three seats, so Frank is the Gallo boy in the fourth seat and John Penn the boy who began in the right end seat. By elimination, Jerry's last name is Parker and the Parton boy's name is Mark. Again by clue 5, after the switch Frank and John had the third and fourth seats from the left respectively. In sum, from left to right:

> Before: Jerry Parker, Mike Bell, Mark Parton, Frank Gallo, John Penn
> After: Mark Parton, Jerry Parker, Frank Gallo, John Penn, Mike Bell

54.   SOCKEY

There is one 17-year-old, a boy (clue 1), one 14-year-old, also a boy (clue 5), and the other four are either 15 or 16 years old. By clue 7, then, the Adler twins are 16, the girl goalie is 15, and Ed is the 17-year-old. Mary is 16, and the Cox boy is the 14-year-old (clue 3); Ed's last name, by elimination, is Burns. Laura's last name is Cox and she is 15 (clue 2). The boys are 14, 16, and 17; by clue 6, Dan is the 14-year-old Cox boy, and the girl who plays wing is 15. The Adler boy, by elimination, is Frank. Since the girl goalie and wing are both 15, the Adler girl is the halfback and is Mary. Nancy's last name, by elimination, is Burns. Since none of the boys is 15, Nancy is the wing and Laura the goalie (clue 4). Ed Burns plays halfback (clue 1). Dan then plays wing (clue 5). By elimination, Frank Adler is the boy goalie. In sum:

154

Halfbacks: Ed Burns, 17; Mary Adler, 16
Goalies: Frank Adler, 16; Laura Cox, 15
Wings: Dan Cox, 14; Nancy Burns, 15

55. TV GAME SHOWS

Neither Wes (clue 1), Sue (clue 2), Tex (clue 3), nor Una (clue 4) won the least amount of money, so Vi did. At least two people won $750 or less—since the largest amount won was $3,000, the person on *Kashword* won $750 at most (clue 1), and the same is true of the person on *Greenback Bonanza* (clue 2). Vi, therefore, who won the least, could not have won more than $750, so the *Pot O' Gold* (clue 3) contestant won no more than $2,250; *Pot O' Gold* was not the top money winner. Neither was *Kashword* (clue 1), *Greenback Bonanza* (clue 2), or *Dollarama* (clue 4); the contestant on *Mr. Moneybags* won $3,000. Sue won $1,500, and the *Greenback Bonanza* contestant $750 (clue 2). Since no two won the same amount, the person on *Kashword* won less than $750. Therefore, Wes didn't win the $3,000 (clue 1), nor did Tex (clue 3); Una did. The contestant on *Dollarama* won $2,000 (clue 4). Sue didn't win her $1,500 on *Kashword* (clue 1), so she won on *Pot O' Gold*. By clue 3, Tex won $750 and Vi $500. Tex was on *Greenback Bonanza* and, by elimination, Vi was on *Kashword*. Wes won $2,000 on *Dollarama* (clue 1). In sum:

> Una won $3,000 on *Mr. Moneybags*
> Wes won $2,000 on *Dollarama*
> Sue won $1,500 on *Pot O' Gold*
> Tex won $750 on *Greenback Bonanza*
> Vi won $500 on *Kashword*

56. ICE-CREAM CONES

There are six possible two-scoop combinations of the three flavors: vanilla-vanilla ($1.00), vanilla-chocolate ($1.05), vanilla-strawberry ($1.10), chocolate-chocolate ($1.10), chocolate-strawberry ($1.15), and strawberry-strawberry ($1.20) each of which was ordered by one of the women. Clue 2 lists four orders which were taken consecutively, the last of which was Susan's. Susan's order was not the last (clue 7), so it was either the fourth or the fifth. If it had been the fourth, then, by clues 2 and 5, the first five orders would have been Ms. Kerr's, Marie's, Alice Burke's, Susan's (costing $1.10), and Ms. Drury's. By clue 7, then, the sixth cone ordered would have cost $1.15 and Ms. Kerr's $1.20. But, by clue 3, Ms. Kerr's was not the most expensive; Susan's order was the fifth. By clue 2, Ms. Kerr's was the second, Marie's the third, and Ms. Burke's the fourth. By clue 5, Alice is Ms. Burke, Susan's cone cost $1.10, and Ms. Drury placed the last order. Ms. Drury's cone was the $1.15 chocolate-strawberry combination, and the first order placed was the $1.20 double strawberry (clue 7). Rose is Ms. Kerr (clue 6). Jane was the first to order (clue 1) and Ms. Drury, by elimination, is Kathy. By clue 3, Ms. Kerr's was the $1.00 double vanilla cone, Ms. Burke's was the $1.05 vanilla-chocolate, and Ms. Filler is Marie and ordered the second $1.10 cone. Since Marie's cone included a scoop of vanilla (clue 5), hers was the vanilla-strawberry, and Susan's was the double chocolate. Jane isn't Ms. Rosten (clue 4), so Susan is, and Jane is Ms. Sense. In sum, in the sequence in which the orders were placed:

> Jane Sense: strawberry-strawberry, $1.20
> Rose Kerr: vanilla-vanilla, $1.00
> Marie Filler: vanilla-strawberry, $1.10
> Alice Burke: vanilla-chocolate, $1.05
> Susan Rosten: chocolate-chocolate, $1.10
> Kathy Drury: chocolate-strawberry, $1.15

57. CLASS REUNION

There are three women among the seven. By clue 1, the first two who arrived—at 1 p.m. and 2 p.m. were Ms. Quinlan and Vera, not necessarily in that order; since Ms. Quinlan isn't Golda, she is Mary. Lon and Mr. Xavier, by clue 2, arrived, in some order, at 5 and 6 p.m. The Bostonian is a woman and she arrived after at least two other men (clue 3), so she is

Golda, and she arrived at 7 p.m.; the other two men then arrived at 3 and 4 p.m. By clue 1, the Atlantan and the Philadelphian are both men; another man is Chicagoan Ibbetson (clue 4), and the fourth is the one from Dallas (clue 3). By clue 4, Ed is the one from Philadelphia. Walters isn't Vera, the Atlantan, the Philadelphian (clue 1), or Golda (clue 7), so he is the Dallas man. Jim, who is neither the Atlantan (clue 1) nor Walters (clue 7), and so is Ibbetson. Rob isn't from Dallas and isn't Mr. Zoltan (clue 3), so he is from Atlanta and is Mr. Xavier, while Mr. Zoltan is Ed. Mr. Walters, by elimination, is Lon. Rob Xavier didn't arrive at 5 p.m. (clue 6) so, by clue 2, he arrived at 6 p.m. and Lon Walters at 5 p.m. Jim Ibbetson arrived at 4 p.m. and Ed Zoltan at 3 p.m. (clue 4). Ullman isn't Golda or the New Yorker and didn't arrive first (clue 5); she is Vera, she arrived second, and New Yorker Mary Quinlan arrived first. By elimination, Golda's last name is Kingston and Vera lives in Houston. In sum:

> 1 p.m.: Mary Quinlan, New York
> 2 p.m.: Vera Ullman, Houston
> 3 p.m.: Ed Zoltan, Philadelphia
> 4 p.m.: Jim Ibbetson, Chicago
> 5 p.m.: Lon Walters, Dallas
> 6 p.m.: Rob Xavier, Atlanta
> 7 p.m.: Golda Kingston, Boston

58. MEAL PLANNING MADE EASY

Each woman planned one meal and no two served the same meal on the same night (clue 1). The five women are Ellen, who planned the meal she served Tuesday (clue 2); Susan, who planned the meal she served Wednesday (clue 3); Karen, who planned the meal she served Friday (clue 4); the one who planned and served meat loaf on Monday (clue 7); and the one who planned and served Thursday's meal. Karen served chili Tuesday (clue 4), so neither Karen, whose meal was Friday (also clue 4), nor Ellen, whose meal was Tuesday (clue 2), planned chili. The one who planned chili prepared stroganoff before Thursday (clue 6), so was not Susan, who served stroganoff Thursday (clue 3). Monday was taken by meat loaf (clue 7), so the chili planner was the one who served it Thursday. Ellen served meat loaf Wednesday (clue 2), and Karen didn't serve meat loaf Monday or Friday (clues 4, 7), so Karen served meat loaf Thursday. Karen's planned Friday meal wasn't stroganoff (clue 6), nor did Susan plan stroganoff (clue 3). Ellen planned and served stroganoff Tuesday. Both Karen and the chili planner served stroganoff two days before they served tuna (clue 6), so one served stroganoff Monday and tuna Wednesday, and the other served stroganoff Wednesday and tuna Friday. Susan's planned Wednesday meal, then, was not tuna; it was spaghetti. By elimination, Karen planned the tuna meal she served Friday, Wednesday's meal was stroganoff (clue 6), and, also by elimination, spaghetti on Monday, which was planned by Ms. Sawyer (clue 4), who is then Susan. The chili planner, then, served stroganoff Monday and tuna Wednesday (clue 6). By elimination, the meat loaf planner served chili Wednesday and stroganoff Friday. Ellen didn't serve tuna Monday (clue 5), so Susan did, and Ellen served chili Monday. Since Karen served tuna on Friday, Ellen served spaghetti and Ms. Landower's tuna casserole Thursday (clue 2). Karen, then, is Landower. Susan, by elimination, served chili on Friday leaving meat loaf for Tuesday, which was planned by Ms. Shoemaker (clue 3). By elimination, the chili planner served meat loaf Friday and spaghetti on Tuesday, while the meat loaf planner served tuna Tuesday and spaghetti Thursday. Ellen is not Ms. White (clue 5), so the chili planner is, and Ellen is Pressley. Ms. White is not Jane (clue 5); she is Marie, and Jane is Shoemaker. In summary (in order from Monday to Friday):

Jane Shoemaker: (planned) meat loaf, tuna, chili, spaghetti, stroganoff
Ellen Pressley: chili, (planned) stroganoff, meat loaf, tuna, spaghetti
Susan Sawyer: tuna, meat loaf, (planned) spaghetti, stroganoff, chili
Marie White: stroganoff, spaghetti, tuna, (planned) chili, meat loaf
Karen Landower: spaghetti, chili, stroganoff, meat loaf, (planned) tuna casserole

59. HIGH SCHOOLS

According to the introduction, each school opened in a different year. Clues 2 and 7 each mention three schools. Jackson High opened thirteen years after another school (clue 2), and the same is true of Jefferson High (clue 7). If, between these two clues, all six schools are named, either Jackson High or Jefferson High would have been the last of the six to open, in 1955 (clue 1). Then, one school would have opened in 1942, contradicting clue 5, so neither Jackson nor Jefferson High Schools opened in 1955. Therefore, the two clues together do not mention all six schools; at least one school is referred to in both clues. Washington High wasn't on Hill Street, because then Jefferson High and Jackson High would have opened the same year. If Lincoln High were on River Street, Jefferson High would be the most-recently opened of the five different schools, and, since we know it was not the last of the six, it would be the fifth. But that contradicts clue 4. If Jackson High were on River Street, that would pose the same contradiction. Only one possibility remains: Jefferson High is on Hill Street. Combining clues 2 and 7, then, the first five schools opened as follows: Washington High, the school on River Street seven years later, Jefferson High on Hill Street six years after that, Lincoln High eight years later, and Jackson High five years after Lincoln. Since we know Jackson High wasn't the last of the six to open, another opened later, in 1955. By clue 3, Madison High can only be the school that opened in 1955, and Jackson High on Glen Street opened in 1951, Lincoln High then opened in 1946, Jefferson High in 1938, the school on River Street, by elimination, Monroe High, in 1932, and Washington High in 1925. By clue 8, Washington High is on Valley Street. The school on Canyon Street is Madison High (clue 6); Lincoln High, by elimination, is on Bay Street. In sum:

> Washington High, Valley Street, 1925
> Monroe High, River Street, 1932
> Jefferson High, Hill Street, 1938
> Lincoln High, Bay Street, 1946
> Jackson High, Glen Street, 1951
> Madison High, Canyon Street, 1955

60.   BICYCLE SAFETY

Each father offered a different combination of safety measures, one of the six possible combinations of the elements listed: a white sweater with either a reflector or white-painted wheels or both; or a fluorescent Sam Browne belt with either a reflector or white-painted wheels or both. The two who suggested three items are fathers of girls (clue 1), while the other four children are boys. Each of the girls accepted two of her father's suggestions (clue 2), so Pat is a boy (clue 3), and the girls are Ann and Lee. The March child, the only one who agreed to both the reflector and wheels, is not Fred (clue 4), and is not Pat (clue 3), Hal (clue 5), Ann, or Ed (clue 7) and must be Lee. Mr. Brown, who suggested the sweater-wheels-reflector combination (clue 6), must be Ann's father, while Mr. March suggested the belt, wheels, and reflector, the last two of which his daughter accepted. Pat and the Jones boy each accepted only one suggestion (clue 3), one of them a reflector and the other a different one (clue 8); Hal and the Sims boy, who were in agreement (clue 5), must have each accepted two suggestions and are respectively the Green boy and Ed (clue 2). Fred is then the Jones boy, and Pat's last name is Drew. Fred then agreed only to the belt (clue 4), so Pat is the one who agreed only to the reflector. Ed Sims' father's suggestions included the sweater (clue 6); since he and Hal Green each rejected one of his father's ideas and took another instead (and no one except Fred accepted the belt), and ended up in agreement, Hal's father did not suggest a sweater and did suggest a belt. Pat's father then was the third one who suggested the sweater, and Ed Sims' father was the one who suggested the sweater plus wheels. Ed and Hal cannot have duplicated Lee March's choice of wheels plus reflector (clue 4), so they chose sweater plus reflector, and the reflector was Mr. Green's second suggestion. By elimination, Fred's father suggested belt plus wheels, and Ann chose the sweater and wheels. In sum:

> Mr. Brown: sweater, wheels, reflector; Ann: sweater, wheels
> Mr. Drew: sweater, reflector; Pat: reflector
> Mr. Green: belt, reflector; Hal: sweater, reflector
> Mr. Jones: belt, wheels; Fred: belt
> Mr. March: belt, wheels, reflector; Lee: wheels, reflector
> Mr. Sims: sweater, wheels; Ed: sweater, reflector

The first to use the magazine did a Logic Problem and wasn't Mr. Brown (clue 4). So, by clue 3, four of the five are the Logic Problem solver, Mr. Brown, the Anacrostic solver, and a person who needed two hours of solving time; and the order in which the last three of these had the magazine was either second, third, and fourth respectively, or third, fourth, and fifth respectively. If their order was third, fourth, fifth, Gary, who was the last to solve a puzzle (clue 2), would have needed two hours, and the crossword, as well as the Anacrostic, would have required one hour of solving time (clues 2 and 3). Everyone needed an hour or more of solving time (clue 5), so Mr. Brown would have needed more than one hour (clue 7) and wouldn't have been the crossword puzzle solver; the crossword would have been the second puzzle done and, as Mrs. Brown didn't solve it (clue 6), she would have been the Logic Problem solver (clue 1). Her solving time was the same as Barbara's (clue 1), who solved either the crossword or the Anacrostic, so it would have been one hour, too. Since all three puzzles would have required one hour, clue 1 would be contradicted. Thus, Mr. Brown was the second user of the magazine, the Anacrostic solver (who needed one hour) the third, a person who needed two hours the fourth, and Gary the fifth and last. Gary did not solve either the Solicross or the expert-level crossword (clue 2), so he did the Word Arithmetic. By clue 1, Mrs. Brown solved the Logic Problem. Since she and Barbara needed the same amount of time, the time for each was either one hour or two hours, so Barbara used the magazine either third, doing the Anacrostic, or fourth, taking two hours. If Barbara had done the Anacrostic, by elimination, Alan would have been the fourth to have the magazine, requiring two hours, and Mr. Brown's time need would have been more than two hours (clue 7). Gary, then, would have needed either twice Mr. Brown's time or twice Alan's time, i.e., four hours or more. So the total time used by the five would have been more than 9½ hours, contradicting clue 5. Thus, Barbara was the fourth to use the magazine, and she and her mother each needed two hours of solving time. Alan, by elimination, was the third to use the magazine. Since Mr. Brown needed more than an hour, his time plus Mrs. Brown's, Alan's and Barbara's was more than six hours; Gary used the magazine for less than three-and-one-half hours (clue 5). His time, then, was double that of the time needed by Mr. Brown rather than double the two hours needed by Barbara. Mr. Brown, then, is the one who did the crossword, and Barbara, by elimination, solved the Solicross. By clue 5, the combined time of Gary and Mr. Brown was 4½ hours. Gary's time was ⅔'s of this, and Mr. Brown's was ⅓ of it; so Gary used 3 hours and Mr. Brown one and one-half hours. In summary, in the order in which the puzzles were done:

> Mrs. Brown: Logic Problem, 2 hours
> Mr. Brown: crossword, 1½ hours
> Alan: Anacrostic, 1 hour
> Barbara: Solicross, 2 hours
> Gary: Word Arithmetic, 3 hours

62. BUTTON WILLOW'S GARDENERS

Each gardener gave two boxes and received two boxes (clue 1); the clues list two white, three yellow, three purple, and two red-flowering bulbs, so no two gave or received identical bulbs. Ann gave a white-flowering bulb to Sabrina (clue 3); since there were only two boxes of white-flowering bulbs, either Ann or Sabrina gave white narcissus and the one who gave the narcissus received white iris bulbs (clue 6). George, then, didn't receive white iris, and neither Jonathan nor Megan gave white narcissus, so George received no white bulbs (clue 2). Since there were only four colors, George (clue 9) gave white iris. Ann, then, gave white narcissus to Sabrina (clue 3), and Ann received the white iris (clue 6). By clue 9, the two bulbs George gave were different from the two he received; so in clue 7, Jonathan, the only other man, received the purple hyacinth and gave the purple crocus bulbs to Sabrina (clue 3). Jonathan, then, didn't give George purple bulbs (clue 9). Megan gave away the same two colors she received (clue 9); by elimination, the only purple bulbs she could receive would be purple iris. Therefore Megan didn't give purple iris to George (clue 2). Megan, then, didn't receive the red tulip bulbs (clue 8). If she received red bulbs, they were red amaryllis, so neither she nor Jonathan, who received a purple-flowering bulb, gave red amaryllis (clue 5) to George. Since George received no purple or white bulbs, he received red (clue 9) tulip bulbs from Jonathan or Megan, and gave away the purple iris bulbs (clue 8). Sabrina didn't give the red amaryllis (clues 3, 5); Ann did. By elimination, Sabrina didn't give red or white bulbs; she gave purple hyacinth and yellow bulbs. Since Ann gave no yellow and Sabrina received no yellow bulbs, Megan gave yellow tulip and received yellow daffodil bulbs (clue 4). By clue 9, Megan must also have given and received red bulbs, so she gave the red tulip to George and received the red amaryllis. George, then, received yellow bulbs from Jonathan (clues 2, 9), which were not tulip or daffodil bulbs (clue 4); they were yellow crocus bulbs. By elimination, Sabrina gave the yellow daffodil bulbs to Megan. Since Ann gave the red amaryllis, she didn't receive the purple iris (clue 5); Ann received the yellow tulip bulbs, and Jonathan received the purple iris. In summary:

Ann gave red amaryllis & white narcissus; received white iris & yellow tulips
George gave purple & white iris; received red tulips & yellow crocus
Jonathan gave purple & yellow crocus; received purple hyacinth & purple iris
Megan gave red & yellow tulips; received red amaryllis & yellow daffodils
Sabrina gave purple hyacinth & yellow daffodils; received purple crocus & white narcissus

63. ALL-STARS

Adding up the years mentioned in clue 2, the three-time all-star had to be in the league at least three years, so Adams was at least six years in the league, and Mickey at least eight. When you subtract that total number of years from thirty (clue 1), there remain at the most thirteen years to divide between two players. Thus, none of the five has been in the league more than twelve years. Of the three people mentioned in clue 2, the three-time all-star has the least time in the league; Edmonds, in clue 9, has less time than he and so is a fourth player. Harry made the all-stars four times (clue 7). Another of the five made the team three times (clue 2), and a third twice (clue 3). The other two have made the team a total of 14 times. No two have made all-star the same number of times, so, the two other numbers of seasons on the all-star team are six and eight or five and nine. Harry has been in the league longer than at least two other players (clue 3); so has Adams (clues 2, 9). The collective years of league membership total thirty (clue 1). Since four players are mentioned in clues 2 and 9, they must overlap the three in clue 3. If Adams were the two-time all-star, then Mickey would be the shortstop. Adams has been in the league at least six years (clue 2), so he cannot be the two-time all-star, since that would bring the total in clue 3 to more than thirty. Since Adams is not the two-time all-star, Mickey is not the shortstop. Adams cannot be the shortstop, since half of his years would equal the time for both the two-time all-star (clue 3) and the three-time all-star (clue 2). Adams' first name is not Mickey (clue 2) nor Harry (clue 7). Thus Harry, Mickey, Adams, the shortstop, and the two-time all-star are five distinct players, and the first three have—in one order or another—been in the league longest. The one in the league the least number of years is then the two-time all-star, the second-least the shortstop (clue 3), and the latter is the three-time all-star (clue 2); the two-time all-star is Edmonds (clue 9). Since no one was an all-star just once, the shortstop is not Kerry (clue 4), nor is he John (clue 6); so he is Len. Len is not Dailey (clue 4) or Barnes (clue 5), so he is Carver. Edmonds' first name is not Kerry (clue 4); it must be John, and Kerry is Adams. Harry is then Barnes, and Mickey's last name is Dailey (clue 7). The most appearances in the all-star games are either five and nine or six and eight. Then, by clue 4, Adams made the all-star team eight times, Dailey six times. The left fielder is not Adams or Dailey (clue 4), or Edmonds (clue 6), so he is Barnes. We know Edmonds was a two-time all-star, so he has been in the league at least two years. When two years is tried in clue 3, then, we find that shortstop Len Carver would be four years in the league and Harry, six years. In clue 2, twice Len Carver's years would be eight years for Kerry Adams and ten for Mickey Dailey. Since these five equal exactly thirty, John Edmonds' years in the league are exactly two. Finally, by clue 8, Dailey is the pitcher, Adams the catcher, and Edmonds the first baseman. In sum, the five, with their years in the league and number of seasons on the all-stars (the latter in parentheses) are:

Catcher Kerry Adams, 8(8)
Left fielder Harry Barnes, 6 (4)
Shortstop Len Carver, 4(3)
Pitcher Mickey Dailey, 10(6)
First baseman John Edmonds, 2(2)

64. MEMORY RETENTION EXPERIMENT

No two of the five students made the same number of correct placements (clue 1); each card was correctly placed by one or more of the five (clue 2); and Gloria made more correct placements than Hal (clue 3). If Bob had gotten all six in the correct order, both Dave and Gloria would have had two cards correctly positioned, while both Eve and Hal would have had one card correctly positioned, contradicting clue 1. Similarly, if any one of the others had all six cards in correct order, we find some combination that contradicts clue 1. So, none of the five correctly positioned all the cards. It is impossible to place five correctly, so the scores were zero, one, two, three, and four cards correctly placed. At least one student placed each card correctly (clue 2), so either the four or the seven was the first card shown. If the seven were correct, then four of the five students would have had at least one card placed correctly; Eve would have been the student with zero correct. Her choice of the three as the last card shown would have been incorrect; three would have been the fifth card shown (the only other position in which it had been placed), and the jack would have been the last card shown. Under these assumptions, Hal would have had the seven, the three, and the jack correctly placed. He made fewer correct placements than Gloria (clue 3), so she would have been the one with four cards correct. Since her ordering of the jack and the three would have been incorrect, the order of her other four cards would have been correct. Her order of these other cards matched Hal's, contradicting clue 3. So, the first card had to be the four. Thus, the seven was the second card shown. Bob and Dave now have three wrong and Gloria and Hal have at least two wrong. Remember, Gloria got more correct than Hal. Gloria and Eve put the next four cards in the same order. If Gloria got all four of her remaining cards in the correct order, then Eve got all six correct, contradicting clue 1. So, Eve was the one with four cards correctly placed. Since Gloria and Eve made matching placements of the last four cards, Gloria got two correct. Since Hal, Gloria, and Eve all made matching placements of the third and fourth cards, and Hal got fewer correct than Gloria, all three were incorrect about the third and fourth cards. Eve and Gloria, then, were both correct about the fifth and sixth placements (the jack and the 3, in that order), and Hal was wrong about both; he was the one who got no correct placements. Bob and Dave both got the sixth card correctly; Bob's fifth card was incorrect. He could not, then, be the one who got three correct; Dave got three correct, and those were the third and fourth cards (the queen and the 9, in that order), while Bob got one correct. In sum, the correct placements are:

Eve:	four	4	7	—	—	j	3
Dave:	three	—	—	q	9	—	3
Gloria:	two	—	—	—	—	j	3
Bob:	one	—	—	—	—	—	3
Hal:	zero	—	—	—	—	—	—

65. FROM A TO Z

Since there were 26 children and grandchildren, by clue 4, the numbers of children were 7, 6, 5, 4, 3, and 1. Adam and Eve, then, had five children, "A" through "E." 17 consonants and four vowels, then, were used by Adam and Eve's grandchildren. The 17 consonants were used by three children, "A," "E," and one child whose name begins with a consonant (clue 6); these children had 7, 6, and 4 children, in some order, while the two other children whose names begin with consonants had three children and one child, and used the four vowels I, O, U, and Y. By clue 1, then, "B" used consonants for his children, and had 7, 6, or 4, while "C" had three children whose names begin with vowels, and "D" had one child whose name begins with a vowel. Since "A," "B," and "E" had, in some order, seven, six, and four children, by clue 7, "E" had four children, "A" had seven, while "B" had six. "D's" child was not "I" (clue 5), "U," or "Y" (clue 2); he had "O." "C's" children, then, were "I," "U," and "Y." "B" did not have "G" (clue 5), so he did not have "F" or "H" (clue 3). "A" did not have "F" (clue 5) so, by elimination, "E" had "F." Since "A" had seven children, but not "F" (clue 5), by clue 3, his first child was either "G" or "H," his second "J" or "K," his third "M" or "N," his fourth "P" or "Q," his fifth "S" or "T," his sixth "V" or "W,", and his seventh was "Z." "B" had three children in sequence, then two of his siblings had at least two children each, after which "B" had three more children (clue 3). These two siblings can only be "A" and "E." "B's" three children in sequence, then, had to be "J," "K," and "L," "K," "L," and "M," or "L," "M," and "N." "A" had either "J"

160

or "K" and either "M" or "N," so "B's" three children in sequence were "K," "L," and "M," while "A" had "J" and "N." "A," then, did not have "H" (clue 3); he had "G." By clue 3, then, his other children were "Q," "T," and "W." By elimination, "H" was "E's" child. "E's" third and fourth children came between "B's" third and fourth children (clue 3), so they were "P" and "R," while "B's" final three children were "S," "V," and "X." In summary:

A: G, J, N, Q, T, W, and Z
B: K, L, M, S, V, and X
C: I, U, and Y
D: O
E: F, H, P, and R

66.   BUT WHERE'S HER HORSE?

There were four squares each of red, blue, green, and yellow. Since no row or column had more than one square of any of these colors (clue 1), four rows and four columns had each of these colors. By clue 2, then, rows 2 and 4 and columns A and D had one square each of red, blue, green, and yellow. The fifth square in these rows and columns was white (clue 1). Row 3 had no red square and column B had no green (clue 8); by clue 1, then, rows 1 and 5 each had a red square, while columns C and E each had a green square. Row 5 also had a green square, and column E had a red square (clue 4). Since there were eight white squares and columns A and D and rows 2 and 4 had only one each, columns B, C, and E had two each, as did rows 1, 3, and 5 (clue 1). There were two blue squares on each diagonal (clue 6). If C-3 were blue, since no two blue squares touched on sides or corners (clue 3), there would be two blue squares in one row or column, contradicting clue 1. C-3 is not blue. By clue 3, the blue squares are either A-1, E-5, B-4, and D-2, or they are A-5, E-1, B-2 and D-4. In either case, columns A, B, D, and E have blue squares, and rows 1, 2, 4, and 5 have blue squares. By clue 1, Row 5 has no yellow square, so the other four rows do (clue 1), and column E has no yellow square, so the other four columns do. Since column B does not have the same combination as row 1 (clue 4), it does not have the fourth red square. Column C, then, has the fourth red square. By elimination, row 3 and column B each have one black square; that square is B-3. The only colors row 5 and column B have in common are white and blue. Since the blue squares are on the diagonals, B-5 is white. A-5 and C-5 are not white (clue 7). Column A has one white square. If that square were A-1, then A-3 would not abut a white square, contradicting clue 5. If A-2 were white, in order for A-4 to abut on a white square, B-4 would be white. B-2, by elimination, would be blue. The blue squares, then, would be A-5, B-2, D-4, and E-1. However, at least one of the two white squares of row 1 would then be abutting another white square around the edge, contradicting clue 7. Since A-2 is not white, but a white square abuts A-1 (clue 5), B-1 is the second white square in column B. B-2, then, is not white; nor are A-1 or C-1 (clue 7). The white square that abuts A-2, then, is A-3. B-2 is either blue or yellow. If it were yellow, then the blue squares would be A-1, B-4, D-2, and E-5. C-1 would not be yellow (clue 3); it would be red. Since column E has no yellow squares, D-1 would be yellow and E-1 white. Since row 5 has no yellow, C-4 would be yellow (clue 3). However, this leaves no place for the yellow square in row 3; B-2 is blue. The blue squares, then, are A-5, B-2, D-4, and E-1. By elimination, B-4 is yellow. The yellow square in row 3 is neither C-3 (clue 3) nor E-3, which has no yellow; it is D-3. By clue 3, the yellow square in row 2 is A-2. By elimination, the yellow square in row 1 is C-1. Since A-1 is not white (clue 7), it is red and, by elimination, A-4 is green and D-1 is white. C-5 is not white (clue 7), so E-5 is. Neither D-5 nor E-4 is white (clue 7), so the white square abutting D-4 is C-4 (clue 5). By elimination, E-4 is red. D-5, then, is not red (clue 3); it is green, and C-5 is red. By elimination, D-2 is red. Two white squares are not yet placed. Exactly two white squares abut, but not on the edge of the picture (clue 7); C-3, then, is white. By elimination, C-2 is green, E-2 is white, and E-3 is green. In summary:

	A	B	C	D	E
1	red	white	yellow	white	blue
2	yellow	blue	green	red	white
3	white	black	white	yellow	green
4	green	yellow	white	blue	red
5	blue	white	red	green	white

67. DETECTIVE DEDUCTION

By clue 5, the six novels are: the one written by Elizabeth, the one set in Rio, "Murder Most Macabre," Mr. Carruthers' novel, the one in which Thomas is the detective, and the one in which Ms. Armstrong is the detective. Since all the first and last names begin with different letters, no author or detective has the same first and last initials. The women detectives are Ms. Trefoyle (clue 4), Ms. Armstrong (clue 5), and Ms. Valentine (clue 8). Vanessa is not Ms. Trefoyle (clue 4), so she is Ms. Armstrong. She appeared in the May selection (clue 4), so Thomas appeared in the June (clue 5). The June book in which Thomas appeared was not "Internationally Intriguing" (clue 3), "Silent Stalker" (clue 7), "Foreign Fatalities" (clue 8), or "Thrilled to Death" (clue 9); it was "Dinner á la Deadly." Its author was not Rosemary (clue 1), Gregory (clue 3), or Ivan (clue 9). The male authors are Mr. Mitchell, Mr. Rockford (clue 3), and Mr. Carruthers (clue 5). Michael is not Mr. Carruthers (clue 6), so (since no author or detective has the same first and last initial) he is Mr. Rockford. Michael, then, did not write the June selection (clue 3); Carmen did. Her last name is not Ellsworth (clue 7) or Garland (clue 9); she is Inwood. Thomas, then, is King, while Michael Rockford's sleuth Banks is Simon (clue 6). By clue 5, either Elizabeth's novel was the January selection, "Murder Most Macabre" the February selection, the one set in Rio March, and Mr. Carruthers' April, or "Murder Most Macabre" was January, Elizabeth's February, Mr. Carruthers' March, and the one in Rio April. In either case, Elizabeth is not Ellsworth (clue 7); she is Garland and, by elimination, Rosemary is Ellsworth. Elizabeth Garland's detective was not Bradley (clue 9); her detective was one of the women. She was not Ms. Trefoyle (clue 9); she was Ms. Valentine. The author of the May selection featuring Vanessa Armstrong was not Rosemary Ellsworth (clue 7); it was one of the male authors. He was not Michael Rockford (clue 6), so he was Mr. Mitchell. Since the novel featuring the detective named Bradley was, at the latest, the April selection, "Silent Stalker" was selected for either January or February (clue 7). That, then, was Elizabeth Garland's novel. Elizabeth Garland's "Silent Stalker" appeared one month before Michael Rockford's book about Simon Banks (clue 9), and before Rosemary Ellsworth's book, which appeared before the one about Bradley (clue 7). By clue 5, then, the order of books is January: Elizabeth Garland's "Silent Stalker" featuring Ms. Valentine; February: "Murder Most Macabre" by Michael Rockford featuring Simon Banks; March: Rosemary Ellsworth's book set in Rio; April: Mr. Carruthers' novel about Bradley; May: Mr. Mitchell's novel featuring Vanessa Armstrong; and June: Carmen Inwood's "Dinner á la Deadly" featuring Thomas King. Since Gregory's novel was not the April selection (clue 3), he is not Mr. Carruthers; Ivan is and, by elimination, Gregory is Mr. Mitchell. "Internationally Intriguing" was neither Ivan Carruthers' April selection nor Gregory Mitchell's May selection (clue 3); it was Rosemary Ellsworth's March selection set in Rio. By elimination, Ms. Trefoyle is Rosemary's detective, while Bradley is Standish. Ivan Carruthers' novel was not "Thrilled to Death" (clue 9); it was "Foreign Fatalities" while, by elimination, "Thrilled to Death" was Gregory Mitchell's novel. Angela was not featured in Elizabeth's January selection (clue 2); Katerina was and, by elimination, Angela was featured in Rosemary's March selection. By clue 2, then, the February selection was set in Moscow and the May selection was set in Istanbul. The novel set in Budapest was not the January (clue 1) nor the April (clue 10) selection; it was the June selection. By clue 3, the April selection was not set in Singapore; it was set in Nairobi, and the January selection was set in Singapore. In summary:

Jan.: Elizabeth Garland's "Silent Stalker," Singapore, Katerina Valentine
Feb.: Michael Rockford's "Murder Most Macabre," Moscow, Simon Banks
March: Rosemary Ellsworth's "Internationally Intriguing," Rio, Angela Trefoyle
Apr.: Ivan Carruthers' "Foreign Fatalities," Nairobi, Bradley Standish
May: Gregory Mitchell's "Thrilled to Death," Istanbul, Vanessa Armstrong
June: Carmen Inwood's "Dinner á la Deadly," Budapest, Thomas King

68. WHO'S ON FIRST—AND IN ROOM 201?

By clue 6, Miss Mills was in room 207, and the girl from Randallstown High was in either 201 or 203. If the girl from Randallstown had shared 203, then Farrah would have shared 205 and Miss Nolan would have been Miss Mills' roommate (clue 9). By clue 3, however, Miss Nolan was not in 207; the girl from Randallstown High, then, was in 201, Farrah shared 203, and Miss Nolan shared 205 (clue 9). The LF shared 201 (clue 8), but she was not the girl from Randallstown High (clue 2); they were roommates. The SS shared 209 (clue 3). The 3B was not the SS's roommate (clue 1), the girl from Randallstown High (clue 2), Farrah (clue 4), Miss Nolan or her roommate in 205 (clue 15); she was either Farrah's roommate in 203 or one of the girls in 207. The girl from Shakespeare High was not in 203 (clue 16) so, by clue 12, the 3B was in 203 and was Farrah's roommate, Bobbi was in 205, and the girl from Shakespeare High was in 207. Miss Nolan is not Bobbi (clue 15), so Bobbi was her roommate. Miss Mills is not from Shakespeare High (clue 10), so the girl from Shakespeare High was her roommate. Abby Lewis shared either 203 or 207 (clue 11). She was not the 3B (clue 4), so she was the girl from Shakespeare High in 207. Jackie, then, was in 201 (clue 11); she was not the LF (clue 20), so she was the girl from Randallstown High. The 1B was in either 205 or 209 (clue 11); she was not in 209 (clue 1), so she was in 205. By clue 1, either the 2B and the 3B were roommates in 203, or the 1B and 2B were roommates in 205. Farrah was not the 2B (clue 14), so the 1B and 2B shared 205. Bobbi was not the 2B (clue 14), so she was the 1B and Miss Nolan was the 2B. By clue 7, the P and RF shared 207. Miss Mills was not the RF (clue 10), so she was the P, while Abby Lewis was the RF. The C from Wildlake High and Gina shared a room, but not 209 (clue 19); they shared 203, and Gina was the 3B while Farrah was the C from Wildlake High. Jackie was not the DH (clue 20); she was the CF and, by elimination, the DH was the SS's roommate in 209. Miss Riley was the SS (clue 13). Since Farrah and Gina shared 203, by clue 17, Darla was in 205 and was Miss Nolan, Heather was in 207 and was Miss Mills, and the Berlin High girl was in 209. SS Riley was not from Berlin High (clue 22); the DH was. Since Heather Mills and Abby Lewis shared 207, Christy was not in 209 (clue 18); she was in 201, and was the LF, while Farrah was Miss James. Erin wasn't the DH (clue 24), so she was SS Riley and, by elimination, the DH was Ingrid. The girl from Easthills High was then in 207 (clue 24); she was Heather Mills. Since none of the girls mentioned in clue 26 was in 207, Miss Scott was in 203, and was Gina. Miss Owens was not in 201 (clue 23); by clue 26, she was in 205, and was Bobbi, while the girl from Ocean City High was in 201, and was Christy. Miss Price and the girl from Vo-Tech shared 209 (clue 25); Erin Riley was from Vo-Tech, while Ingrid was Miss Price. Jackie was not Miss Quinn (clue 21); she was Miss Kelly while, by elimination, Christy was Miss Quinn. The girl from Fillmore High was neither Bobbi Owens (clue 23) nor Gina Scott (clue 26); she was Darla Nolan. Gina Scott was not from Central High (clue 5); she was from Glenecho High while, by elimination, Bobbi Owens was from Central High. In summary:

201: Christy Quinn, LF from Ocean City High and Jackie Kelly, CF from Randallstown High
203: Farrah James, C from Wildlake High and Gina Scott, 3B from Glenecho High
205: Darla Nolan, 2B from Fillmore High and Bobbi Owens, 1B from Central High
207: Heather Mills, P from Easthills High and Abby Lewis, RF from Shakespeare High
209: Erin Riley, SS from Vo-Tech High and Ingrid Price, DH from Berlin High

69. BROWN'S DAIRY

The number of black cows plus the number of black/white cows equals ten, as does the number of brown cows plus the number of brown/white cows; in addition, there is a different number of each color (clue 6). Clue 2 lists four cows of different colors, as do clues 4 and 10; there are at least three cows of each color. By clue 11, then, there are seven black cows, three black/white cows, and either four brown/white cows and six brown cows or three brown/white cows and seven brown cows. By clue 8, there are an even number of brown cows, so there are six brown cows and four brown/white cows. Karen, a spotted cow, is in stanchion 14 (clue 12). Stanchions 7 and 8 contain the same color cows; they are either black or brown (clue 5). If they were brown, then 18 and 19 would also contain brown cows (clue 8), which would contradict clue 5. Stanchions 7 and 8, then, contain black cows, while 10 also contains a black cow and stanchions 6 and 9 contain brown cows (clue 5). Stanchions 20 and 17 also contain brown cows (clue 8). The fifth brown cow is on side A, while the sixth is in the stanchion opposite on side C, and both are in even-numbered stanchions (clue 8). They are, then, in stanchions 4 and 12. There are a total of seven spotted cows, none on side B. By clue 13, then, the other three sides contain one, two, and four spotted cows, in some order. Side C contains at least two spotted cows, in stanchions 13 and 14 or 14 and 15 (clue 12). If side A contained four spotted cows, two pairs of cows would be in opposite stanchions—14 and 2, and either 3 and 13 or 1 and 15—contradicting clue 13. Side C, then, contains four spotted cows; these are in stanchions 11, 13, 14, and 15. Side A, then, can only contain one spotted cow (clue 13), so side D contains two. By elimination, Side A contains three black cows, while Side D contains one black cow. Since two black cows cannot be next to each other (clue 5), black cows are in stanchions 1, 3, and 5, while stanchion 2 contains a spotted cow. The only side containing all four colors is Side D; Betty, Jewel, Lola, and Rose are on this side (clue 4). The fifth cow on this side is mentioned in clue 2; by clue 1, it is neither Alice nor Iris, so the fifth cow on side D is either Elsie or Odette. Cora and Dora are not on the same side (clue 1) so, by clue 10, Cora is in the last stanchion on one side, while Dora, Flora and Nora are in the first three stanchions on the next; Cora is in either 5 or 10. Since they are of all different colors (clue 10), Cora is not in 5; she is in 10, Dora in 11, Flora in 12, and Nora in 13. Alice, then, is in 15 (clue 12). The side C cows are neither in alphabetical nor reverse-alphabetical order; by clue 3, then, sides B and D are. Since Cora is in stanchion 10, that is the side in reverse-alphabetical order, while side D is in alphabetical order. Betty, then, is in stanchion 16 and Rose in 20. Betty is black (clue 9), so the cows in stanchions 18 and 19 are spotted. By clue 7, Gertrude, Paula, and Toni are all black cows and are on side A. By clue 1, Hester, Queenie, and Sandra are not on that side; they are on side B. The fifth cow on side B is mentioned in clue 2; it is not Iris (clue 1), so it is either Elsie or Odette. In either case, Sandra is in stanchion 6 and Queenie in 7 (clue 3). Toni is a black cow on side A so, by clue 7, she is in either 3 or 5. If she were in 5, two stalls from Queenie, then Hester would be in 8 and Paula in 4. However, Paula is also a black cow, so she is not in 4. Toni, then, is in stanchion 3, and is four stanchions from Queenie. By clue 7, then, Paula is eight stanchions from Hester; Paula is in stanchion 1 and Hester in stanchion 9. Gertrude, the third black cow on side A, is in stanchion 5. The fifth cow on side B, then, comes alphabetically between Hester and Queenie; that cow is Odette, in stanchion 8. The fifth cow on side D, then, is Elsie (clue 2); she is in stanchion 17, Jewel is in 18, and Lola is in 19 (clue 3). By elimination, Iris and Monica are, in some order, in stanchions 2 and 4. Since Jewel is a spotted cow, Iris is also (clue 9); Iris is in stanchion 2, while Monica is the brown cow in stanchion 4. Jewel and Iris are the same color (clue 9), as is Karen (clue 13). Neither Alice nor Nora, then, are the same color as Karen (clue 5), so Alice and Nora are the same. Dora is not the same as Nora (clue 10); she matches Karen, Iris, and Jewel. There are only three black/white cows, so they are not that spotted color; Dora, Karen, Iris, and Jewel are brown/white, while Alice and Nora are black/white. By elimination, Lola is also black/white. In summary:

1. Paula, black
2. Iris, brown/white
3. Toni, black
4. Monica, brown
5. Gertrude, black
6. Sandra, brown
7. Queenie, black
8. Odette, black
9. Hester, brown
10. Cora, black
11. Dora, brown/white
12. Flora, brown
13. Nora, black/white
14. Karen, brown/white
15. Alice, black/white
16. Betty, black
17. Elsie, brown
18. Jewel, brown/white
19. Lola, black/white
20. Rose, brown

70. NIFTY NAPKINS

The party with five guests was not for the graduation (clue 1), birthday (clue 4), or first novel (clue 7); it was for either the anniversary or the welcome home. By clue 4, either Yvonne's party had five guests and the party with the rabbit napkins had either eight or twelve, or the party with the rabbit napkins had five guests and Yvonne's had either eight or twelve. The anniversary party was neither Yvonne's nor the one with rabbit napkins (clue 8); it was not the party with five guests. The party with five guests, then, was for the welcome home. The woman who had twenty guests was not Yvonne (clue 4), Carly (clue 5), or Jody (clue 7); she was either Wallis or Mallory. If she had been Wallis, her napkins would not have been the bishops' caps (clue 1), swans (clue 3), rabbits (clue 4), or ducks (clue 6); they would have been the pineapples. Her party would not have been the anniversary (clue 2), graduation (clue 3), or novel (clue 9); it would have been the birthday. The woman who had fifteen guests, then, would not have been Yvonne (clue 4), Carly (clue 5), or Jody (clue 7); she would have been Mallory. Her napkins would not have been bishops' caps (clue 1), rabbits (clue 4), or ducks (clue 6); they would have been swans. Her occasion would not have been the graduation (clue 3) or novel (clue 9); it would have been the anniversary. The woman who had the cap napkins would not have been Jody (clue 7) or Yvonne (clue 8); she would have been Carly. Yvonne would not have had the rabbit napkins (clue 4); Jody would have,

164

while Yvonne's would have been ducks. The novel party would not have been Carly's (clue 5) or Jody's (clue 7); it would have been Yvonne's. Yvonne, then, would have had more than five guests; by clue 4, the welcome home party with five guests would have featured rabbit napkins by Jody. Carly's party with cap napkins would not have had twelve guests (clue 1); Yvonne's novel party with duck napkins would have, while Carly's with bishops' caps would have had eight guests. By elimination, Carly's party would have been for the graduation. This, however, would contradict clue 1; Wallis did not host the party with twenty guests. Mallory, then, hosted that party. Her napkins were not bishops' caps (clue 1), rabbits (clue 4) ducks (clue 6), or pineapples (clue 9); they were swans. Since Mallory did not give the party for the novel (clue 9), the woman who had fifteen guests was not Yvonne (clue 4) or Jody (clue 7); she was either Wallis or Carly. If she had been Wallis, her napkins would not have been rabbits (clue 4) or ducks (clue 6). Since Mallory did not give the graduation party (clue 3), Wallis's napkins would not have been bishops' caps (clue 1); they would have been pineapples. Her occasion would not have been the anniversary (clue 2), graduation (clue 3), or novel (clue 9); it would have been the birthday. Yvonne and the woman who had the rabbit napkins, then, would have had, in some order, five and eight guests (clue 4). Mallory's party, then, would not have been for the graduation (clue 3) or novel (clue 9); it would have been for the anniversary. The woman who had cap napkins was neither Jody (clue 7) nor Yvonne (clue 8); she would have been Carly. Her party, then, would not have had twelve guests (clue 1); Jody's would have. This, however, would contradict clue 7. Wallis, then, did not have fifteen guests; Carly did. Her napkins were not bishops' caps (clue 1), pineapples (clue 2), or rabbits (clue 4); they were ducks. The woman who had the cap napkins was neither Jody (clue 7) nor Yvonne (clue 8); she was Wallis. Yvonne did not have the rabbit napkins (clue 4); Jody did while, by elimination, Yvonne had the pineapple napkins. Since the woman who gave the novel party was neither Carly (clue 5) nor Mallory (clue 9), Jody did not have twelve guests (clue 7). Either Yvonne or Jody with rabbit napkins had five guests (clue 4). If Yvonne had had five guests, Jody would have had eight while, by elimination, Wallis would have had twelve. The novel party would not have been Carly's (clue 5), Jody's (clue 7), or Mallory's (clue 9); it would have been Wallis's. The graduation party would not have been Mallory's (clue 3); by clue 1, then, it would have been Carly's. By clue 4, then, the birthday party would have been Mallory's so, by elimination, the anniversary party would have been Jody's. This, however, would contradict clue 8; Yvonne did not have five guests at her party. The party with five guests, then, had rabbit napkins (clue 4), and was Jody's. If Yvonne had had eight guests, Wallis would have had twelve. Yvonne's party would not have been for the graduation (clue 1), birthday (clue 4), or novel (clue 9); it would have been for the anniversary. This, however, would contradict clue 2; Yvonne did not have eight guests. Wallis, then, had eight guests at her party with bishops' caps napkins while, by elimination, Yvonne had twelve at her party with pineapple napkins. By clue 4, then, the birthday party had twenty guests, and was Mallory's. The novel party was neither Carly's (clue 5) nor Yvonne's (clue 9); it was Wallis's. The anniversary party was not Yvonne's (clue 2); it was Carly's while, by elimination, Yvonne had the graduation party. In summary:

> Carly, ducks, anniversary, fifteen
> Jody, rabbits, welcome home, five
> Mallory, swans, birthday, twenty
> Wallis, bishops' caps, first novel, eight
> Yvonne, pineapples, graduation, twelve

71. GULLIBLE'S TRAVELS

We know Gullible left the fifth country he visited on a ship; he left Altupa on the shoulders of an angry mob (clue 1), Tullipil in a hot-air balloon (clue 2), Tat II's domain on a log raft (clue 5), and the land of the foolish magicians on an elphant (clue 7). The Tullipil citizens were not the intelligent bovines (clue 2), the pedagogues, or the 400-lb.'ers (clue 6); they are the matchstick-thin people. King Tat II's people are not the 400-lb.'ers (clue 8), so they are either the pedagogues or the bovines. If they were the bovines, the Altupa natives would have been the 400-lb.'ers (clue 1) and, by elimination, the fifth country's natives would have been the pedagogues. Altupa, then, would have been the fourth country visited (clue 1). By clue 5, then, Oldaag would not have been the fifth country visited; it would have been the third, and would have been the land of foolish magicians, while Tat II's domain would have been visited second (clue 5), and Tullipil first (clue 2). Moomador's land, then, would have been visited fourth (clue 7), and would have been Altupa. By clue 3, Mayor Jingleheimer's land would have been visited first, and Tat II's domain would have been Bordingbang; by elimination, Monshynhuh would have been the fifth country. Dramaticus, then, would have ruled either the land of the foolish magicians or Monshynhuh; this, however, would contradict clue 4. King Tat II's people, then, are not the intelligent bovines; they are the pedagogues, and their land was visited just after Altupa (clue 1). Thus, the order of the countries is: Altupa, then King Tat's land of teachers and, by clue 5, Oldaag is next. If Altupa had been the first country visited, Oldaag, then, would have been the land of foolish magicians. By elimination, Tullipil would have been visited fourth; the fifth country, then, would have been the land of the bovines (clue 2) while, by elimination, Altupa would have been the land of the 400-lb.'ers. Moomador's land would have been visited fourth (clue 7), and would have been Tullipil. By clue 3, Mayor Jingleheimer's land would have been Altupa, while Tat II's domain would have been Bordingbang. By elimination, the fifth country visited would have been Monshynhuh. Again, however, Dramaticus's land would have been either the land of the foolish magicians or Monshynhuh, contradicting clue 4. Altupa, then, was not the first country visited. If Tullipil's thin people had been the first visited, the land of the bovines would have been second (clue 2); that land would have been Altupa, followed by King Tat's kingdom of teachers and then Oldaag, which would have been the land of the foolish magicians (clue 7). Also by clue 7, then, Moomador's land would have been the last one visited. The leader of the fourth country would have been neither Dramaticus (clue 4) nor Queen Leeahh (clue 10); he would have been Mayor Jingleheimer. By clue 3, then, Bordingbang would have been the fifth country visited, and, by elimination, the land of the 400-lb.'ers. This, however, would contradict clue 9; Tullipil was not the first country visited. By elimination, the first country visited was the land of the magicians. Since Gullible left Tullipil by balloon (clue 2), that was not the last country he visited. By clue 5, then, Oldaag is the last country visited, while Tat II's domain was the fourth. Altupa, then, was the third (clue 1) so, by elimination, Tullipil was the second. Altupa, then, is the land of the intelligent bovines (clue 2) while, by elimination, Odaag is the land of the 400-lb.'ers. Moomador was the leader of Tullipil (clue 7). By clue 3, Bordingbang was visited fourth and Mayor Jingleheimer's land was Altupa. By elimination, the first country visited was Monshynhuh. Dramaticus was not the leader of Monshynhuh (clue 4); he was leader of Oldaag while, by elimination, Leeahh was the leader of Monshynhuh. In summary:

1. Monshynhuh, Leeahh, magicians, elephants
2. Tullipil, Moomador, thin, balloon
3. Altupa, Jingleheimer, bovines, mob
4. Bordingbang, Tat II, pedagogues, raft
5. Oldaag, Dramaticus, 400-lb.'ers, sailing ship

72. THE SAFE-HOUSE PROJECT

Paula, a woman on Teakwood Place, and Ms. Fenwick all rode to the meeting in Ms. Fenwick's car (clue 1). Trudy drove by herself (clue 6). Three women, Leah, Ms. Breck, and a woman on Linden Way, all rode bikes (clue 9). Flo picked up Ms. McCrea (clue 3), while Beth picked up Ms. Garen (clue 10). These, then, are eleven of the twelve women. Six women live on each side of Central Avenue; the three bike riders live on the west side (clue 9), while Paula, the woman on Teakwood, and Ms. Fenwick all live on the east side (clue 14). Beth, who drives directly past Ms. Garen's house on the way to the meeting (clue 10), lives on Magnolia in #6 or on Ash in #9 or #10. Frances drove to the meeting (clue 7), so she is either Ms. Fenwick or the twelfth woman. Since all other women are accounted for, if Frances is the twelfth woman, she drove by herself. In either case, then, she drove directly from her house (clue 1). Since she made three turns to get to the meeting from her house (clue 7), she lives in #6, #9, or #10. Ms. Agner also drove to the meeting (clue 7); she is not Flo (clue 3) or Trudy (clue 12), so she is either Beth or the twelfth woman. If she were the twelfth woman, she drove to the meeting alone. She would, then, live in either #6, #9, or #10 (clue 7), and Frances would be Ms. Fenwick. Ms. Fenwick lives on the east side, so Frances Fenwick would live in #6, while Ms. Agner and Beth would live, in some order, in #9 and #10 on the west side. Ms. Garen (clue 10) and Trudy (clue 12), then, would also live on the west side. This, however, would give a total of seven women on the west side. Ms. Agner, then, is not the twelfth woman; she is Beth. Beth, Ms. Garen (clue 10), Trudy (clue

12), and Ms. Reid (clue 6) all live on the same side of Central Avenue. If they lived on the east side, Trudy and Ms. Reid would live in #2 and #3 on Juniper (clue 6); Beth would live in #6 and Ms. Garen in #1 (clue 10). However, this would leave no place for Ms. Kozak, who lives in either #1 or #6 (clue 8). Beth, Ms. Garen, Trudy, and Ms. Reid, then, all live on the west side. By elimination, Ms. Reid is either the woman on Linden who biked or Leah, while Flo, Ms. McCrea, and the twelfth woman all live on the east side. Frances, who is either Ms. Fenwick or the twelfth woman, then lives on the east side; she lives in #6 on Magnolia (clue 7). By clue 8, then, Ms. Kozak lives in #1 on Palm. Ms. Slayton and Louise live side by side (clue 5). Trudy is not Ms. Slayton (clue 6), so Ms. Slayton is either the bike rider from Linden or Leah. Louise, then, who lives on the same street as Ms. Slayton, is not a bike rider (clue 9); she is Ms. Garen. Louise Garen does not live on Ash (clue 10); she lives on Linden in either #11 or #12. Ms. Slayton, then, is the bike rider from Linden. By elimination, then, Ms. Reid is Leah. Trudy and Leah Reid live on Dogwood in #7 and #8 (clue 6). By clue 9, then, Ms. Breck lives on Ash in either #9 or #10. By elimination, Beth Agner is the second woman who lives on Ash, in either #9 or #10. We know that Frances lives in #6 on Magnolia while Ms. Kozak lives on Palm in #1. By the map, the woman who lives on Teakwood and walked to Ms. Fenwick's lives in either #4 or #5. By clue 3, then, Flo lives in either #2 or #3 on Juniper, while Ms. McCrea lives on Teakwood in either #4 or #5. Leah and Trudy live on the same street, so Trudy is not Ms. Truitt (clue 13). She lives in either #7 or #8, so the woman who lives in the house one number higher is Leah Reid, Ms. Breck, or Beth Agner; she is, then, not Ms. Horne (clue 11). Since the only woman who could possibly live north of Trudy is Leah Reid, Trudy is not Ms. Cushing (clue 4). Trudy is Ms. Wiggins. By clue 11, then, Trudy Wiggins lives in #7, Ms. Horne lives in #6 and is Frances, while Leah Reid lives in #8. Frances Horne, then, is the twelfth woman. By clue 1, Ms. Fenwick lives in either #2 or #3 on Juniper. By elimination, Ms. Kozak, who lives on Palm in #1, is Paula. Flo is not Ms. Truitt (clue 3); she is Ms. Cushing while, by elimination, the woman on Teakwood who walked to Ms. Fenwick's is Truitt. By clue 13, Ellen lives on the north side of Teakwood, so she is Ms. McCrea, and lives in #5, while Ms. Truitt lives in #4. June lives on the east side (clue 4), but is not Ms. Truitt (clue 13); she is Ms. Fenwick. June Fenwick and Flo Cushing both live on Juniper so, by clue 4, Flo Cushing lives in #2 while June Fenwick lives in #3. June lives in #3 and Ellen in #5, so Ms. Truitt, who lives in #4, is neither Bella nor Esther (clue 2); she is Bonnie. Bella and Esther, then, are in some order Ms. Slayton and Ms. Breck. Ms. Slayton lives in either #11 or #12, while Ms. Breck lives in either #9 or #10; by clue 2, then, Bella is Ms. Slayton, and she lives in #11, while Esther is Ms. Breck, and she lives in #10. By elimination, then, Beth Agner lives in #9, while Louise Garen lives in #12. In summary:

1: Paula Kozak, Palm, driven by Ms. Fenwick
2: Flo Cushing, Juniper, drove Ms. McCrea
3: June Fenwick, Juniper, drove Ms. Truitt and Ms. Kozak
4: Bonnie Truitt, Teakwood, driven by Ms. Fenwick
5: Ellen McCrea, Teakwood, driven by Ms. Cushing
6: Frances Horne, Magnolia, drove alone
7: Trudy Wiggins, Dogwood, drove alone
8: Leah Reid, Dogwood, biked
9: Beth Agner, Ash, drove Ms. Garen
10: Esther Breck, Ash, biked
11: Bella Slayton, Linden, biked
12: Louise Garen, Linden, driven by Ms. Agner

73. GLOVES, HATS, AND SHOES

Ten pairs of gloves, ten hats, and ten pairs of shoes were sold, for a total of 30 items. No one bought more than one item per department and no two shopped in the same three departments (clue 1). There are only ten possible combinations—boys'-girls'-women's, boys'-girls'-men's, boys'-girls'-shoes, etc.—so each department sold six items. Each clerk sold at least one of each item (clue 1), so the most anyone sold of any item was four. The shoe department sold four pairs of shoes (clue 14), one hat, and one pair of gloves to total six. The girls' department sold three pairs of shoes and one pair of gloves (clue 15) plus two hats to total six. Seven pairs of shoes are accounted for, so the other three departments each sold one pair. Underwood sold at least two pairs of shoes (clue 5), but wasn't in the shoe department (clue 13), so she had the girls' department, and Young, who sold at least two pairs of shoes (clues 3, 8), had the shoe department. Underwood sold two hats and one pair of gloves, so the boys' department sold three hats (clue 13) plus two pairs of gloves to total six, and the women's department sold three pairs of gloves (clue 14) plus two hats to total six. The men's department, then, sold three pairs of gloves and two hats to total ten each. Wendell sold three hats (clue 15), so had the boys' department—the only one which sold three hats. If Vance had the women's department, he'd have sold no shoes at all (clue 12), so Vance had men's, and Tindall had women's. Items for young boys and girls were found only in the boys' and girls' departments respectively (introduction), so Carolyn bought gloves in boys' and a hat in girls' (clue 2). She didn't buy shoes from Tindall (clue 2) or Vance (clue 12), so she bought shoes from Young in the shoe department. King is a man and got a hat in boys' and shoes in girls' (clue 2); since no two shopped in the same three departments, he didn't get gloves in the shoe department (clue 1), or from Tindall (clue 2); he got them from Vance. King is not David (clue 7), Henry (clue 8), or Charles (clue 10). Vance sold no shoes to Charles (clue 5), Brian (clue 6), David (clue 7), Henry (clue 8), or any woman (clue 12), so his one pair of shoes was sold to Adam, who bought a hat from Wendell (clue 4). Adam, then, is not King, so Brian is. Adam is not Owens (clue 3), Parker or Nolan (clue 4), Queen (clue 5), Smith (clue 6), Lattimer (clue 7), Jones (clue 8), or Miller (clue 9). Adam is Ressler. Vance sold only one pair of gloves to a woman (clue 12), so he sold two to men, one of whom was Brian King (clue 6); the other was not to Adam (who bought shoes), David (clue 7), or Charles (clue 10). Henry bought gloves from Vance. Charles, who bought shoes from Underwood (clue 5), is not Owens (clue 3), Queen (clue 5), Smith (clues 6, 10) Jones (clue 8), Miller (clue 9), or Parker (clues 9, 10). If Charles were Nolan, he'd have bought a hat from Wendell (clue 4), shoes from Underwood, and gloves from Young (clue 10). Those were the departments Carolyn used, so Charles isn't Nolan (clue 1); he is Lattimer. Beverly, who bought gloves from Underwood and a hat from Young or Vance (introduction, clue 11), is not Nolan (clue 4), Queen (clue 5), Smith (clue 6), Miller or Parker (clue 9), or Jones (clue 11). She is Owens, who bought shoes from Young (clue 3) and a hat from Vance. Carolyn isn't Nolan (clue 4), Queen (clue 5), Smith (clue 6), Miller or Parker (clue 9); she is Jones. Henry, who bought gloves from Vance and shoes from Young (clue 8), isn't Queen (clue 5), Smith (clue 8), Parker or Miller (clue 9). He is Nolan, who bought a hat from Wendell (clue 4). Angela bought gloves from Tindall and isn't Miller or Parker (clue 9), nor is she Smith (clue 6). Angela is Queen and bought the third pair of shoes from Underwood (clue 5). Tindall sold one pair of shoes, but not to Beverly Owens or Helen (clue 3), Carolyn Jones (clue 8), Angela (clue 9), or to any man (clue 12). Diane bought shoes from Tindall. She is not Miller or Parker (clue 9), so she is Smith, who bought gloves from Vance (clue 6). Helen bought shoes from Young (clue 3), so she isn't Miller (clue 9). David is Miller and Helen is Parker who bought gloves from Tindall (clue 9). David Miller bought a hat from Tindall and shoes from Wendell (clue 9). Since Beverly is the only one who bought gloves from Underwood (clues 11, 14), and David didn't buy gloves from Vance in the men's department (clue 7), David bought the only gloves Young sold. Charles bought gloves from Wendell (clue 10), and Adam, then, bought the third pair of gloves Tindall sold. Since Carolyn bought from Wendell, Underwood, and Young, Charles Lattimer, who bought from Wendell and Underwood, did not buy his hat from Young (clue 1) or Vance in men's (clue 7); Charles bought the second hat Tindall sold. The three hats Wendell sold went to Adam, Brian, and Henry, so Diane Smith, who didn't buy anything from Underwood (clue 7), and bought gloves from Vance (clue 6), bought the only hat Young sold. Since Angela bought shoes from Underwood, she bought the second hat Vance sold, and Helen bought her hat from Underwood. In summary:

Ms. Tindall, women's
Ms. Underwood, girls'
Mr. Vance, men's
Ms. Wendell, boys'
Mr. Young, shoes
Carolyn Jones: gloves (boys'), hat (girls'), shoes (shoes)
Brian King: gloves (men's), hat (boys'), shoes (girls')
Charles Lattimer: gloves (boys'), hat (women's), shoes (girls')
David Miller: gloves (shoes), hat (women's), shoes (boys')
Henry Nolan: gloves (men's), hat (boys'), shoes (shoes)
Beverly Owens: gloves (girls'), hat (men's), shoes (shoes)
Helen Parker: gloves (women's), hat (girls'), shoes (shoes)

Angela Queen: gloves (women's), hat (men's), shoes (girls')
Adam Ressler: gloves (women's), hat (boys'), shoes (men's)
Diane Smith: gloves (men's), hat (shoes), shoes (women's)

74. DOG DAYS

By clue 2, six of the dogs, from lowest-numbered run to highest, were: the Dalmatian, a dog brought in Saturday, Ranger, Mr. Owens' dog, a dog brought in Wednesday, and Edna's dog. By clue 9, six of the dogs, from lowest-numbered run to highest, were: Henry's, Ms. Nolan's, the German shepherd, a dog brought in Tuesday, Donna's, and Mr. Strang's. Since there were only ten dogs, at least two dogs must be mentioned in both these clues. If Donna owned the Dalmatian and Mr. Strang brought his dog in on Saturday, then Henry's dog would have been in the first run and Edna's in the last. This, however, would contradict clue 1. If Henry brought his dog in on Wednesday and Edna was Ms. Nolan, the ten dogs would have been, from lowest to highest run: the Dalmatian, a dog brought in Saturday, Ranger, Mr. Owen's dog, Henry's dog, which he brought in Wednesday, Edna Nolan's dog, the German shepherd, a dog brought in Tuesday, Donna's dog, Mr. Strang's dog. By clue 1, then, the beagle would have been in run 10, and been Mr. Strang's, while Carol would have owned the Dalmatian. By clue 8, then, since Duke's run number has to be half of Betty's, Duke would have been in run 4 or 5. If he were in run 5, Betty's dog would have been in run 10 with Mr. Strang's dog; if Duke were in run 4, Betty's dog would have been in run 8, leaving no room for Frank and Ivan, contradicting clue 8. If Henry were Mr. Owens, Ms. Nolan brought her dog in Wednesday, and Edna owned the German shepherd, then nine of the dogs would have been, from lowest to highest run: the Dalmatian, a dog brought in Saturday, Ranger, Henry Owens' dog, Ms., Nolan's dog, which she brought in Wednesday, Edna's German shepherd, a dog brought in Tuesday, Donna's dog, and Mr. Strang's dog. This, however, would leave no place for Betty's, Frank's, and Ivan's dogs in adjacent runs, contradicting clue 8. By elimination, then, nine of the dogs, from lowest to highest run, are: Henry's, Ms. Nolan's, the German shepherd, the Dalmatian brought in Tuesday, Donna's dog brought in Saturday, Mr. Strang's dog Ranger, Mr. Owen's dog, a dog brought in Wednesday, and Edna's dog. By clue 8, Betty's dog is in an even-numbered run numbered 4 or higher; since Frank's, Betty's, and Ivan's dogs were in adjacent runs (clue 8), the first run that can accommodate this scenario is if Betty brought her dog in on Wednesday and the even number for that run must be 8. Since Edna's dog was, then, in run 9, Frank's and Ivan's dogs were in runs 6 and 7, in some order. Mr. Owens, whose dog was in run 7, is not Ivan (clue 2); he is Frank, and Mr. Strang is Ivan. By clue 8, Duke was in run 4. The dogs in the first nine runs, then, were: Henry's, Ms. Nolan's, the German shepherd, the Dalmatian named Duke brought in Tuesday, Donna's dog brought in Saturday, Ivan Strang's dog Ranger, Frank Owens' dog, Betty's dog brought in Wednesday, and Edna's dog. By clue 1, then, Carol's dog was in the 10th run, while the beagle was in the first, and was Henry's. By clue 12, John Trent owned the German shepherd, which he brought in Thursday. By elimination, Alice is Ms. Nolan, while George owns Duke the Dalmatian. By clue 5, Henry is Mr. Rodman and John Trent's shepherd is King. George is Mr. Lang. By clue 4, Henry owned Lucky. By clue 11, the Newfoundland was Ivan's dog so, by clue 4, the pointer was Frank's. Ms. McGee did not bring her dog in on Saturday (clue 6), so she was not Donna; so, Ms. McGee is one of the women whose dogs were in the last three runs. Since there are two runs between each dog in clue 6, the setter was not in one of the last three runs. It was not brought in on Saturday (clue 6), so it was not Donna's dog. The setter, then, was Alice Nolan's dog. By clue 8, then, Princess was in run 5, and was Donna's dog. Alice's setter was not Tiny (clue 4), Zippy or Spot (clue 6), or Missy (clue 10); it was Blaze. Since Ms. McGee's dog was in one of the last three runs and Spot had to be more than two runs away, she was Carol, and Spot was in run 7, and was Frank's (clue 6). Betty is not Ms. Quail (clue 8), so her dog was not Missy (clue 10), nor was it Tiny (clue 4); it was Zippy. By clue 10, then, Edna Quail's dog was Missy, while, by clue 4, Tiny was in run 10. Donna, whose dog was brought in Saturday, is not Ms. Upham (clue 3); she is Ms. Perkins and, by elimination, Betty is Ms. Upham. Donna owns the collie (clue 10). Since there were ten dogs in all, by clue 3, three dogs were brought in Thursday, one on Saturday, and two on Tuesday, Wednesday, and Friday. Since Donna's Princess, then, was the only dog brought in Saturday, and since Alice's setter Blaze was not brought in Thursday (clue 3), she brought her setter in Wednesday, Carol McGee brought her Tiny in Tuesday, and Spot was brought in on Thursday (clue 6). Of the three remaining dogs, two were brought on Friday and one on

169

Thursday; Ivan did not bring his Ranger on Thursday (clue 7); he brought Ranger on Friday. In clue 3, Blaze came in on Wednesday, George's Duke on Tuesday, and Ms. Upham's Zippy on Wednesday; the Spitz, then, came in Friday. It was, then, neither Betty's nor Carol's dog; it was Edna's. By elimination, Henry's dog came in Thursday. By clue 4, the Weimaraner was Betty's Zippy so, by elimination, Carol's dog was the Great Dane. In summary:

1. Beagle, Lucky, Henry Rodman, Thursday
2. Irish setter, Blaze, Alice Nolan, Wednesday
3. German shepherd, King, John Trent, Thursday
4. Dalmatian, Duke, George Lang, Tuesday
5. Collie, Princess, Donna Perkins, Saturday
6. Newfoundland, Ranger, Ivan Strang, Friday
7. Pointer, Spot, Frank Owens, Thursday
8. Weimaraner, Zippy, Betty Upham, Wednesday
9. Spitz, Missy, Edna Quail, Friday
10. Great Dane, Tiny, Carol McGee, Tuesday

75. GOLF SCRAMBLE

The married couples are the Listers (clue 1), the Parkers (clue 5), and the Monroes (clue 9). Neither Sandra nor Karen are Mrs. Lister or Ms. Field (clue 12), and Dawn isn't Field (clue 7), so Judy is, and Dawn is Lister. Larry is married, but not to Dawn Lister (clue 1) or Sandra (clue 10); he is Monroe or Parker, so his wife isn't Judy Field; it is Karen. Mrs. Parker had no best shots on the 8th hole (clue 5) and Sandra had three (clue 10), so Sandra is not Parker. She is Monroe, and Karen and Larry are the Parkers. Bob is married (clue 9), and is not Monroe (clue 15), so he is Lister. Mr. Smith had one final putt (clue 3); Chester had two (clue 11), so Chester is not Smith. Chester is Monroe, and Arnold is Smith. Larry and Karen Parker were on the same team (clue 1). Since neither Arnold nor Mrs. Parker were on the team whose members had a best shot on each hole (clue 5), Arnold was on the Parkers' team. The fourth team member was a Lister (clue 1), but not a man (also clue 1), so was Dawn Lister. The others formed the second team. With nine holes and two teams, there were 18 best tee shots and 18 final putts. Men made 12 of the best tee shots—two each on three holes and one each on six holes (clue 8)—and women made six. Women had 12 final putts—two each on four holes and one each on four holes (clue 8), and men made six. Judy had two best tee shots (clue 2), and Sandra Monroe had one (clue 9), so Bob and Chester had three each (clue 18) to total nine for their team. Dawn (Bob's wife) had one best tee shot (clue 9), so Karen had two to total six for the women (clue 8), Arnold Smith had three (clue 3), and Larry had three to total nine for his team. Arnold had one final putt (clue 3), and Karen and Dawn both had an even number (clue 19); to total nine for the team, Larry had to have an even number. If Larry had four, Dawn had eight (clue 19)—too many! Thus, Larry had two and Dawn had four (clue 19), so Karen had two to total nine for her team, and Bob had one (clue 19). With Judy's four final putts (clue 2), Chester's two (clue 11), and Bob's one, Sandra had two to total nine for her team. On Judy's team, each player had a best shot on each hole (clue 5), so the minimum score for any hole was four. On Dawn's team, all but the 4th and 8th holes had a minimum of four strokes (also clue 5). Holes 3 and 5 were tied at five strokes each (clue 6). Dawn's team played first on the 2nd and 5th holes (clue 7), so they won the 1st and 4th holes (introduction). Judy's team played first on the 4th and 7th holes (clue 7), so they won the 2nd hole (since the third was tied) and the 6th. Since losers have the *highest* score, Judy's team scored five or more on the 1st hole and Dawn's team scored five or more on the 2nd and 6th. Dawn's team won one hole by 7–3 (clues 5, 13), either the 4th or 8th (clue 5); it was not the 4th (clue 20), so was the 8th. Scores on all other holes had to be 4, 5, or 6 (clue 13), so Dawn's team won the 4th hole 4–6 (clue 20). On the 7th hole, Dawn's team scored six—two of Larry's, two of Dawn's, plus the tee shot and the final putt (clue 14), so Sandra's team won it with five (clue 17). We now know each team won three holes, two holes were tied, leaving only the 9th hole to be determined. The team that scored 45 points won the 9th hole (clue 6) and lost the game by three strokes (clue 21), for a final score of 42–45. A subtotal of the scores already ascertained plus minimum scores of four for holes won or unknown and five for holes lost, shows Judy's team has 45 and Dawn's team has 41. Thus Dawn's team won the game and Judy's team won the 9th hole 4–5. Neither Arnold (clue 5) nor either woman had the best tee shot on the 4th hole for their team (clue 8); Larry did. Arnold Smith didn't have the best tee shot on the 7th hole (clue 3), nor did Larry or

170

Dawn Lister (clue 14); Karen did. Neither Bob, Chester Monroe, nor Sandra had the final putt for their team on the 4th hole (clue 15); Judy did, so a man on the other team had the final putt (clue 8); it was not Arnold (clue 5), so was Larry, and he was the fifth (and only man) to have the best tee shot and final putt on the same hole (clue 12). Neither Karen (clue 16) nor either man (clue 8) had the final putt on the 1st hole for their team; Dawn did. On the 1st hole, neither Dawn (Bob's wife—clue 9) nor Karen (clue 16) had the best tee shot; a man did, so a woman on the other team had the best tee shot (clue 8); it was not Sandra Monroe (clue 9); it was Judy. Karen and a man had the best tee shots on the 7th hole (clue 8); Bob didn't (clue 18), so Chester did. Thus Chester didn't have the final putt on the 7th hole (clue 12) nor on the 4th (Judy's), the 1st, 2nd, 5th, or 8th holes (clue 8). Chester's team won both the 6th and 9th holes, so he final putted only one of those (clue 11) plus the 3rd hole (also clue 11), on which he did not have the best tee shot (clue 12). Sandra Monroe, then, didn't have the best tee shot on the 6th hole (clue 9), the 2nd, 4th, or 8th holes (clue 8), the 1st, 3rd, or 9th holes (clue 9), or the 7th (which Chester took). Sandra's one best tee shot was on the 5th hole, so Chester had the best tee shot on the 2nd hole (clue 9). Since Sandra Monroe had only one best tee shot (clue 9), the fifth hole must have also been one of her final putts (clue 12). Dawn's one best tee shot was after the 4th hole (clues 8, 9), but not on the 7th (Karen's), or the 8th (clue 8) holes. Since Bob Lister didn't have the best tee shot on the 2nd or 6th holes (clue 18), Dawn Lister's was not on the 5th or 9th (clue 9). It was on the 6th, and Bob had the best tee shot on the 3rd hole (clue 9). Since Dawn had only one best tee shot (clue 9) she must have had the final putt for her team also on the 6th hole (clue 12). Since Dawn had only one best tee (clue 9), Karen, then, had the best tee shots on the 3rd hole (clue 8). Dawn and a man had the best tee shots on the 6th hole (clue 8); Bob did not (clue 18), so Chester did, and his three best tee shots are now placed. Chester's other and only winning putt was not on the 6th hole (clue 12), so was on the 9th, and Bob had the best tee shots for his team on the 4th and 8th holes (clue 8). Bob's three best tee shots are now placed, so Judy and a man had the best tee shots on the 9th hole (clue 8); Arnold Smith didn't (clue 3), so Larry did. Likewise, Larry's was the best 8th hole tee shot. Arnold, then, had the best tee shots for his team on the three remaining holes—1st, 2nd, and 5th. Arnold's final putt was after the 5th hole and before the 9th (clue 3), so was on the 7th. Karen's two consecutive final putts (clues 4, 5) can only be on the 2nd and 3rd holes. Neither man (clue 8) had the final putt on the 5th or 8th hole, so Dawn did. All but Larry's final putts are placed for his team, so Larry, by elimination, final putted the 9th hole to make it the only hole on which two men had the final putts (clue 8). Also by clue 8, then, all the other putts were made by a man and a woman. Chester's two putts are already in place, so Bob is the man on the 6th hole who made the final putt with Dawn. On the 7th hole the woman with Arnold was not Sandra (clue 17), so it was Judy. The only hole on which Judy could have had both the best tee shot and the final putt (clue 12) was the 1st. Of the four holes which Judy's team won, Bob final putted the 6th, Judy the 7th, and Chester the 9th, so Judy's second winning putt (clue 2) was on the 2nd hole, and Sandra's second final putt, by elimination, was on the 8th. In summary:

Judy's team: Judy Field, Bob Lister, Chester & Sandra Monroe
Dawn's team: Dawn Lister, Karen & Larry Parker, Arnold Smith

HOLE	SCORE Judy's Team	SCORE Dawn's Team	Best Tee Shots	Final Putts
1	5	4	Judy & Arnold	Judy & Dawn
2	4	5	Chester & Arnold	Judy & Karen
3	5	5	Bob & Karen	Chester & Karen
4	6	4	Bob & Larry	Judy & Larry
5	5	5	Sandra & Arnold	Sandra & Dawn
6	4	5	Chester & Dawn	Bob & Dawn
7	5	6	Chester & Karen	Judy & Arnold
8	7	3	Bob & Larry	Sandra & Dawn
9	4	5	Judy & Larry	Chester & Larry
TOTAL	45	42		